Wonders of Learning

DISCOVER

SHARKS

Dive into the deep blue sea and learn about the life of sharks!

Published by North Parade Publishing Ltd.
4 North Parade, Bath, BA1 1LF, England.

Designed and packaged by
Q2A Creative
Printed in China

DISCOVER
SHARKS

Contents

A Shark's Tale

Sharks are amongst the most feared creatures on Earth, and only the very brave dare to go near them. They are meat lovers and have been around since before even the dinosaurs! Found in oceans, seas and rivers, they rule the waters with their sharp teeth and swift movements. Sharks are related to fish, yet they differ in many ways.

Dorsal fin

Bony matters

While most fish have skeletons made of bones, the shark skeleton is made up entirely of cartilage. Cartilage is the same flexible material that is found inside your ears and nose. It makes the shark lighter in weight and helps it to swim faster.

Long pointed snout

First dorsal fin

Second dorsal fin

Symmetrical Caudal fin

Gill slits

Pectoral fir

Barbel

Pectoral fin

Most fish have bony skeletons

Living dens

Sharks can be found in most oceans and seas Large and more active sharks usually stay nea the surface or the middle of the ocean. Th smaller ones prefer the ocean floor. Som sharks live near the coast and can e enter rivers and lakes that linked to the sea.

FACT FILE

Known species
Over 350
The biggest
Whale shark: can grow up to
18 m (59 feet) long
The smallest
Pygmy ribbontail catshark:
20 cm (8 inches) long
The fastest
Shortfin mako: swims at
about 35 km/h (21.75 mph)
The longest-living
Spiny dogfish: 70-100 years

■ Remoras attach themselves to sharks and take a free ride with them. They also feed on crumbs of food that fall off a shark's mouth

Size matters

Sharks come in all sizes and shapes. Some are tiny, and can easily fit into the palm of your hand. Others, such as the whale shark, can grow to a length of 18 m (59 feet) and can weigh over 18,000 kg (39,683 pounds) – almost twice as much as an elephant!

Pelvic fin

Anal fin

■ Cartilage is elastic in nature, making the shark skeleton flexible. This helps sharks to turn around quickly

Asymmetrical
caudal fin

INTERESTING FACT!

Shark skin is so tough that in the past, people dried it and used it as sandpaper! It was called shagreen. In Germany and Japan, shark skin was once also used on sword handles for a non-slip grip.

Skin that protects

Sharks have a special skin cover. Unlike the overlapping scales of fish, shark skin is covered with small, tooth-like scales. These are called denticles. These protect sharks and make the skin very hard and rough.

In the Beginning...

Most creatures go through evolution, or change their features to adapt to their environment. But sharks are good survivors and have had little need to change in the last 150 million years.

Few fossils

Fossils are the dead remains of animals that stay preserved for hundreds of millions of years. Fossils have helped us study evolution. But a shark's skeleton crumbles quickly, as it is made of cartilage. Complete shark fossils, therefore, have not been found. All the fossils that have been found have been limited to their teeth and spines from their fins.

■ The Helicoprions lived 250 million years ago. Their jaws had a spiral-tooth setting, with smaller teeth on the front and larger ones at the back

Earliest sharks

Scientists believe that the ancestors of modern-day sharks appeared 350 to 400 million years ago, a time known as the Age of Fish, or the Devonian Period. This was 100 million years before dinosaurs existed. The earliest shark fossils are found in Antarctica and Australia.

INTERESTING FACT!

It is believed that extinct sharks had short, round snouts, while most modern sharks have long and pointed snouts. Some even have saw-like snouts.

■ The Orthacanthus lived in fresh waters and had V-shaped teeth. This species is now extinct

FACT FILE

MEGALODON
Tooth size
Around 15 cm
(6 inches) long
Was found around
Europe, India,
Australia, America
Weighed
Over 35 tons (77,162
pounds), equal to the weight
of 12 elephants
Length
More than 16 m (52.5 feet)
Jaws opened up
1.8 m (6 feet) wide and
2.1 m (7 feet) high

■ A Megalodon tooth

■ A full-grown
human, standing
at 1.8 m (6 feet),
would have been
just as big as the
Megalodon's fin

The mega monster

One extinct shark known for its huge fossil teeth is the Megalodon.
It lived between 25 and 1.6 million years ago. Each of the
Megalodon's teeth was the size of a full-grown person's hand!
Scientists believe it was probably longer than 16 m (52.5 feet). It may
have been similar in appearance to the great white shark and is
thought to have fed on whale meat.

Modern sharks

Most modern-day sharks stopped evolving a long time ago. They have changed
very little in the last 100 million years. But scientists are still not sure about how
many kinds of sharks exist today. They continue to discover new species.

Body Basics

Living in the water can be tough. To meet this challenge, sharks are equipped with special features. All sharks have strong jaws, a pair of fins and nostrils and a flexible skeleton. Sharks are great swimmers but, unlike fish, they cannot move backwards.

Colouring effect

Shark skin is double shaded, with the top side being darker than the belly. When the shark is seen from above, its upper surface appears to resemble the dark ocean floor. Seen from below, the belly blends in with the light above. This helps the shark to hunt without being noticed.

INTERESTING FACT!

A shark's tongue is very different from a human one. Found on the floor of the mouth, it is small, thick and mostly still. It is called a basihyal. Some sharks use it to rip the flesh off their prey.

■ The anatomy of sharks varies according to their habitats. Sharks living in deeper oceans have larger eyes than those found near the ocean surface

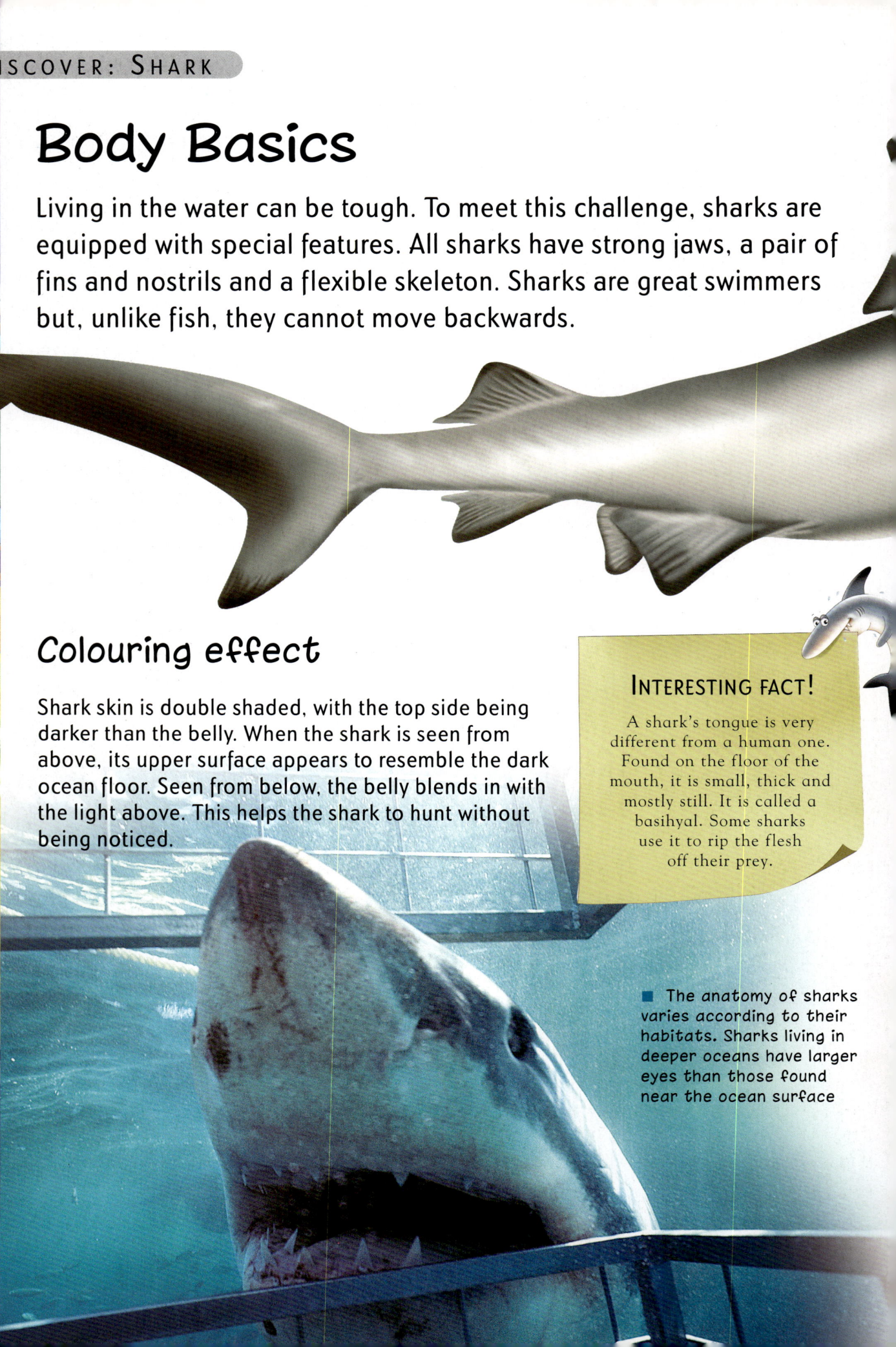

■ Unlike the gills of bony fish, shark gills do not have covers. Water must continue to flow across the gill slits for the shark to breathe

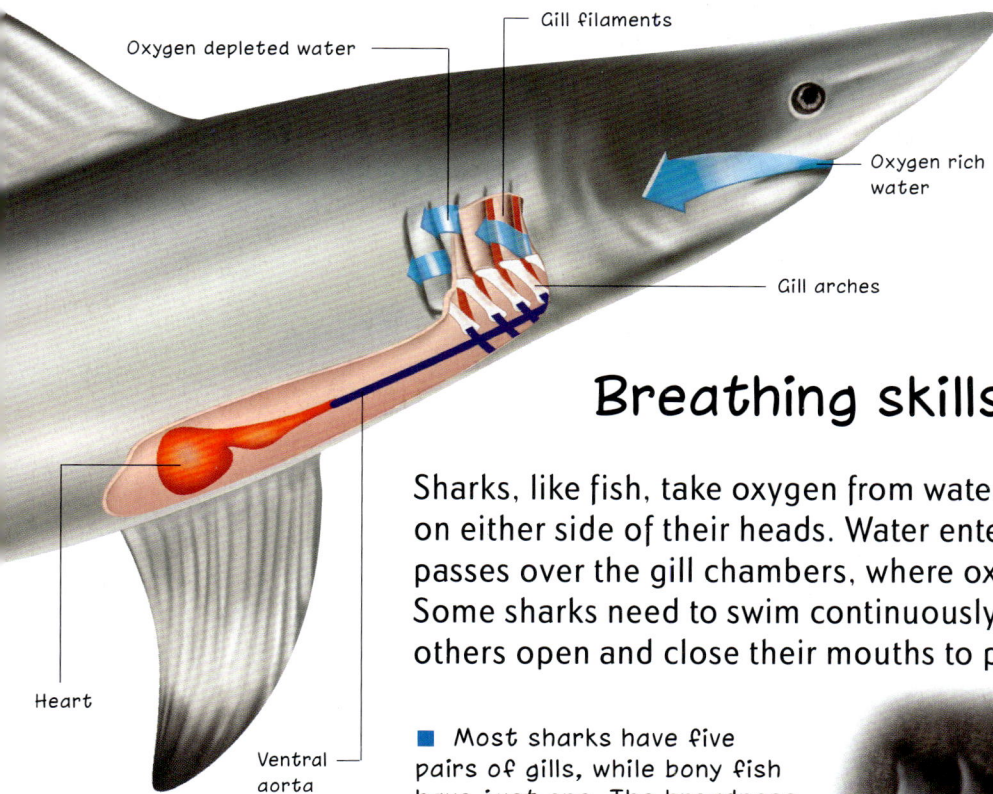

Oxygen depleted water

Gill filaments

Oxygen rich water

Gill arches

Heart

Ventral aorta

Breathing skills

Sharks, like fish, take oxygen from water. They have gill slits on either side of their heads. Water enters these slits and passes over the gill chambers, where oxygen is absorbed. Some sharks need to swim continuously to breathe, while others open and close their mouths to pump the water in.

■ Most sharks have five pairs of gills, while bony fish have just one. The broadnose sevengill shark, however, has seven pairs of gills

Oil Tank!

The largest organ in a shark is the liver, which is filled with oil. Since oil is lighter than water, it keeps the shark from sinking. Despite this, sharks must swim constantly to keep afloat. The liver also functions as a storehouse of energy.

Torpedo-like!

Most sharks have a rounded body that tapers at both ends. This torpedo-like shape helps them while swimming. But some sharks, like the angelshark, have a flat body. This helps them to live at the bottom of the ocean.

■ Sharks usually have blunt snouts. But sawsharks have long snouts with toothed edges, which help them to dig out prey from the ocean floor or to slash at fish passing by

■ The unique shape of the hammerhead shark's head helps it to get a better view of its surroundings

Shark Senses

Sharks have all the senses that humans do – and something extra too! Sharks can not only smell, see, feel, hear and taste. They also have a sixth sense. Their senses help them to hunt and travel great distances.

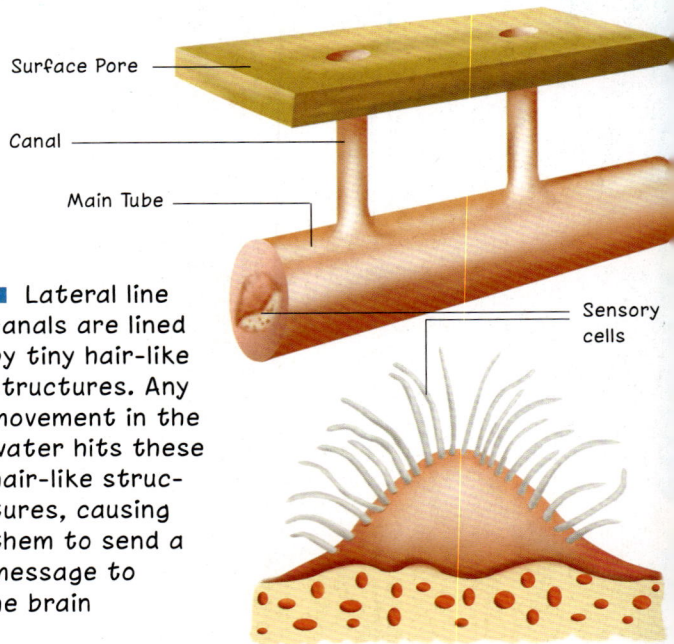

Surface Pore
Canal
Main Tube
Sensory cells

■ Lateral line canals are lined by tiny hair-like structures. Any movement in the water hits these hair-like structures, causing them to send a message to he brain

Line of action

Sharks have fluid-filled canals that run from head to toe on both sides of their body. This is called the lateral line. It enables the shark to sense movements in water. Some scientists believe that the lateral line can also detect low sounds.

Sixth sense

While electricity usually comes from wires and batteries, all living creatures also produce weak electric fields. Sharks are able to detect these with the help of their sixth sense. Tiny pores on the shark's snout lead to jelly-filled sacs known as the ampullae of Lorenzini that help them detect electrical fields

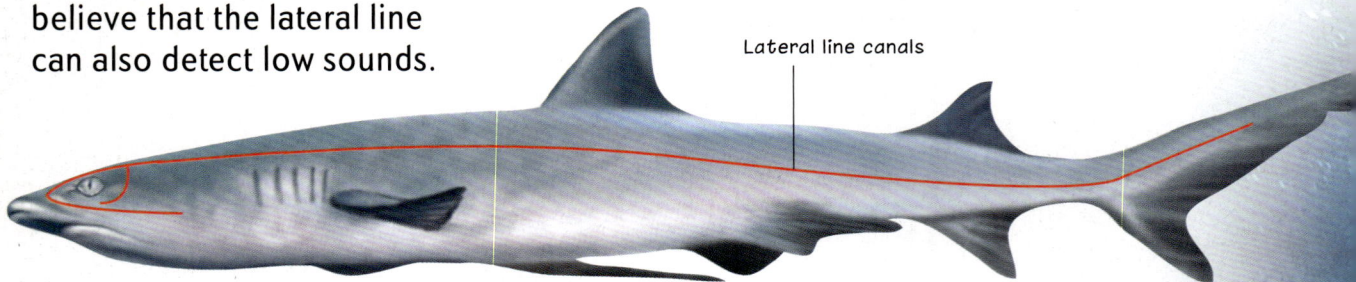

Lateral line canals

Smelly matters

In general, the nostrils of sharks are located on the underside of their snouts. They are used for smelling and not for breathing. Some sharks have nasal barbels, which look like thick whiskers sticking out from the bottom of the snout. Barbels help the shark to feel and taste.

■ Blind sharks cannot see. They hunt for their prey by using their nasal barbels

■ Certain sharks, such as the nurse shark, have openings called spiracles just behind their eyes. The shark uses these spiracles to breathe while hunting or feeding

Looking on

Sharks have very good eyesight, even better than ours. A shark's eye, like that of a cat, can contract or expand according to the light. This helps them to see in dim light. Sharks can also see colours.

INTERESTING FACT!

Sharks do not have external ear flaps. Instead, their ears are inside their heads, on both sides of the brain case. Each ear leads to a small pore on the shark's head.

■ The great white shark has a keen sense of smell. It can detect a drop of blood in 100 litres (176 pints) of water!

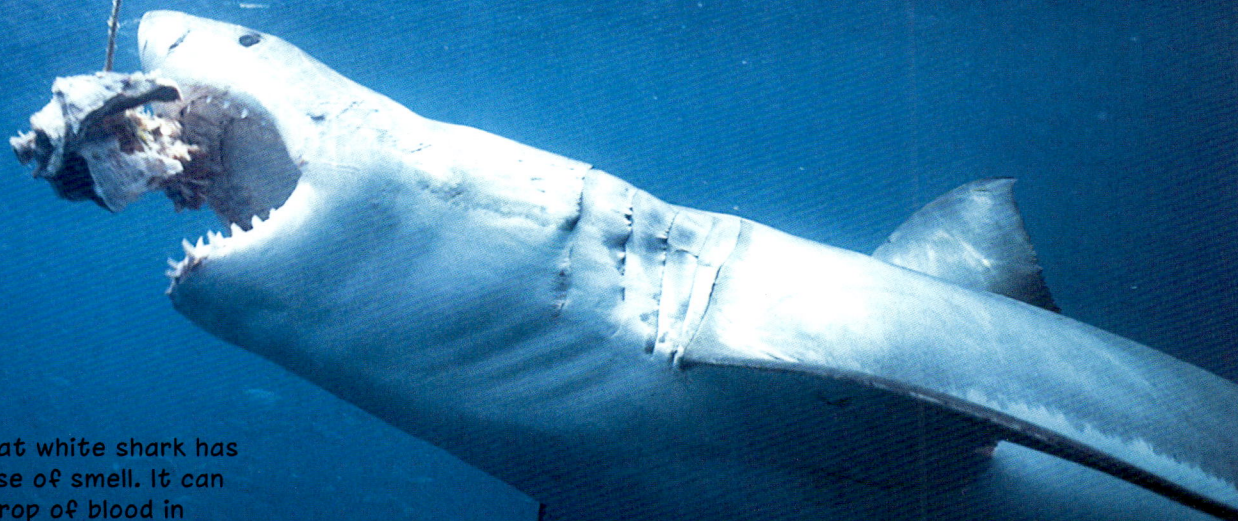

Toothy Terrors

A shark's only proper weapon is its mouth. The mouth is below the snout in all species except the angelshark, the megamouth, whale shark and wobbegong shark. These species have their mouths at the end of their snouts. The two most important parts of a shark's mouth are the teeth and the jaws.

Great white shark

Tearing and crushing

Sharks do not chew their food, but gulp it down whole. They use their teeth only to tear the food into mouth-sized pieces. Some sharks also crush the shell of their prey with their teeth.

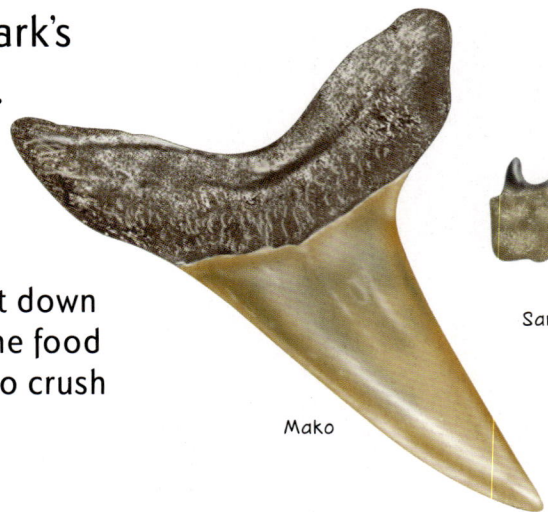
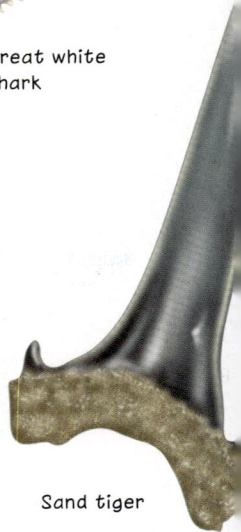

Sand tiger

Mako

Big bite

In most animals, the lower jaw moves freely, but the upper jaw is attached to the skull. However, in sharks, the upper jaw rests below the skull. It moves out when the shark attacks its prey. This allows the shark to push its entire mouth forward to grab its victim. As the lower jaw teeth puncture and hold the prey, the upper jaw teeth slice it.

■ Different types of shark teeth

■ The great white has large wedge-shaped teeth with jagged edges. The teeth of the Megalodon were three times larger than those of the great white

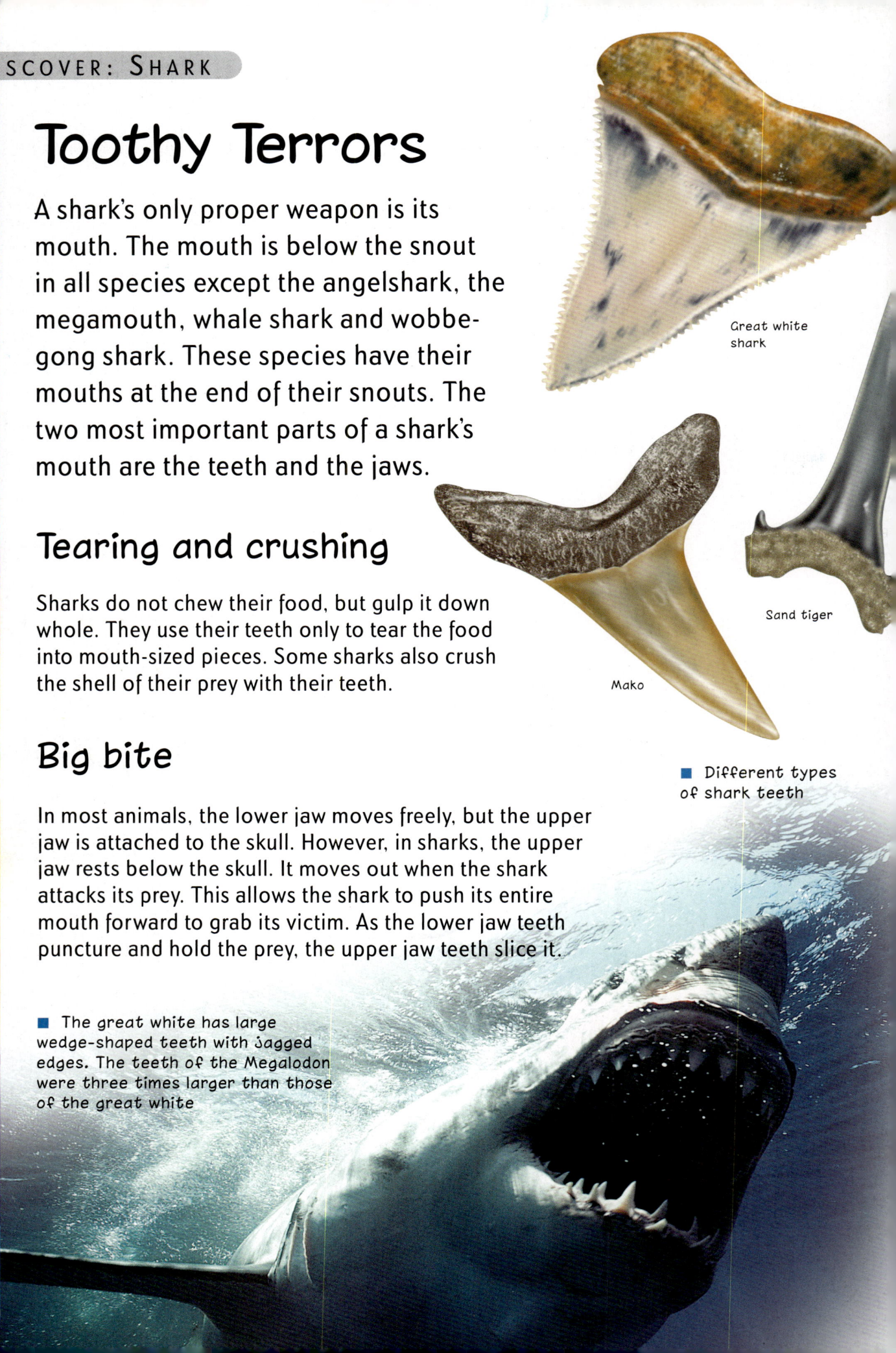

Hammerhead

Blue shark

Sharp new ones

Shark teeth fall out all the time. This is crucial, as worn out or broken teeth are continually replaced by new and sharper ones. The process takes place as often as every two weeks. In some sharks, like the great white, these teeth are arranged in several rows.

Tooth types

Sharks have a variety of teeth. Some have molar-like teeth, which help in the process of grinding. Others have razor-like cutting or pointed teeth.

■ Cookie-cutter sharks eat their prey by attaching themselves to it with special sucking lips. Once attached, they roll their body to cut out a chunk of flesh!

INTERESTING FACT!

The basking shark has very tiny teeth. It does not use them to feed. Instead, the shark swallows plankton-rich water. Special bristles inside its mouth, called gill rakers, filter this food as the water flows through them.

■ The Port Jackson shark does not have jagged teeth. Its front teeth are pointed for grasping its prey, while the back teeth are flat and molar-like for crushing

Young Ones

Baby sharks are called pups. A single litter could contain more than 100 pups! There are three different ways in which shark pups are born.

Laying eggs

Some sharks lay eggs like birds. The mother deposits the egg cases in the sea. The baby inside the egg gets its food from the yolk until the egg hatches. The parents do not protect the eggs. Horn sharks and swell sharks are egg-laying sharks. Such sharks are known as oviparous sharks.

Birth of a shark

Sharks like the hammerhead give birth to pups. The eggs hatch inside the mother's body and the babies get their food from the mother directly. Sharks that give birth to their young in this manner are called viviparous sharks. Lemon sharks, hammerheads, bull sharks and whale sharks are all types of viviparous sharks.

■ Horn shark eggs are spiral shaped and hatch six to nine months after being laid. The pups are usually 15-17 cm (5.9-6.7 inches) long

■ Certain shark's eggs are also called mermaid's purses because of their pouch-like appearance. The egg contains yolk that the baby feeds on

Hatching inside

In some sharks, although the eggs hatch inside the mother, the young ones do not get nourishment directly from their mother. Instead, the babies feed off other unfertilised eggs. At times, they even eat up their brothers and sisters! This kind of reproduction is called ovoviviparity.

■ A shark giving birth. The newborn pup lies on the ocean floor for a while after it's born. It then pulls against the cord that links it to its mother. Once the cord breaks, the young one swims away

FACT FILE

Pups can take nine months to two years to be born
At a time, 2 to 135 young ones are born
Largest egg 36 cm (14 inches)
Largest litter Blue shark: 135 pups
Average life span 25 years, though some can live for up to 100 years

INTERESTING FACT!

Shark eggs are enclosed in a tough leathery membrane. They can be of various shapes – pouch-like or shaped like a screw. Some even have tendrils that attach themselves to seaweeds and rocks on the ocean floor.

Caring for babies

Sharks do not care for their babies. The young sharks are well-equipped to look after themselves. In fact, they swim away from their mothers as soon as they are born. Sometimes a mother can even eat her newborn pups.

■ The predators of young sharks include larger sharks and killer whales. Some small sharks are even eaten by huge fish like the giant grouper

Giants of the Deep

Huge sharks have dominated the oceans of the world for centuries. Although the largest sharks today do not compare in size to the Megalodon they can still grow to enormous sizes. Amongst the modern sharks, the largest are the whale shark and basking shark.

Not a whale!

Contrary to what its name suggests, the whale shark is not a whale. It is a shark that can grow to the length of a bus! The whale shark has a huge mouth that may measure up to 1m (4 feet).

Straining food

Whale sharks and basking sharks feed on plankton by straining the tiny marine plants and animals from the water. They swim with their mouth open and suck in water filled with plankton. The shark then filters its food through special bristles attached to the gills and swallows the food. The water is ejected through the gill slits.

INTERESTING FACT!

Both whale sharks and basking sharks are slow swimmers. They swim by moving their body from side to side. Neither of these sharks is a danger to humans.

Whale shark

Colourful skins

Whale sharks have light-grey skin with yellow dots and stripes. On the other hand, basking sharks are darker in colour. They are greyish-brown to black or bluish on the upper surface, while their belly is off-white in colour.

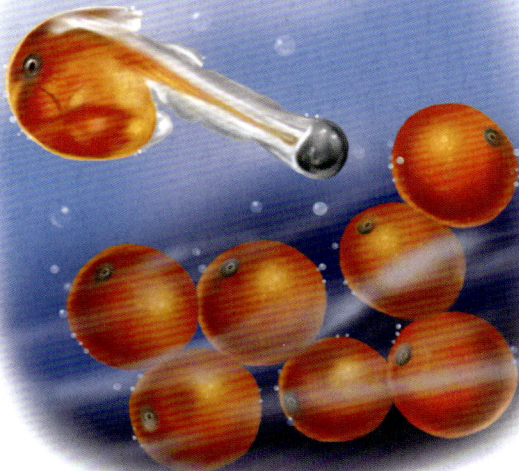

■ Whale sharks love fish eggs. They are known to wait for hours for fish to lay eggs so that they can eat them. They even return year after year to the same mating grounds where the fish release their eggs into the water

The big basking

The basking shark is the second-largest shark. It has a short and conical snout. Unlike whale sharks that travel alone, basking sharks often move around in schools of 100 members.

■ Basking sharks are so called because they cruise slowly along the ocean surface. This gives them the appearance of basking in the sun

Pygmies of the Deep

Not all sharks are huge monsters. Some are, in fact, so small that they can fit into your hand! The smallest sharks include the pygmy ribbontail catshark, dwarf lanternshark and the spined pygmy shark. But like their bigger siblings, small sharks have strong teeth, and a bite from them can be decidedly painful!

Whale shark

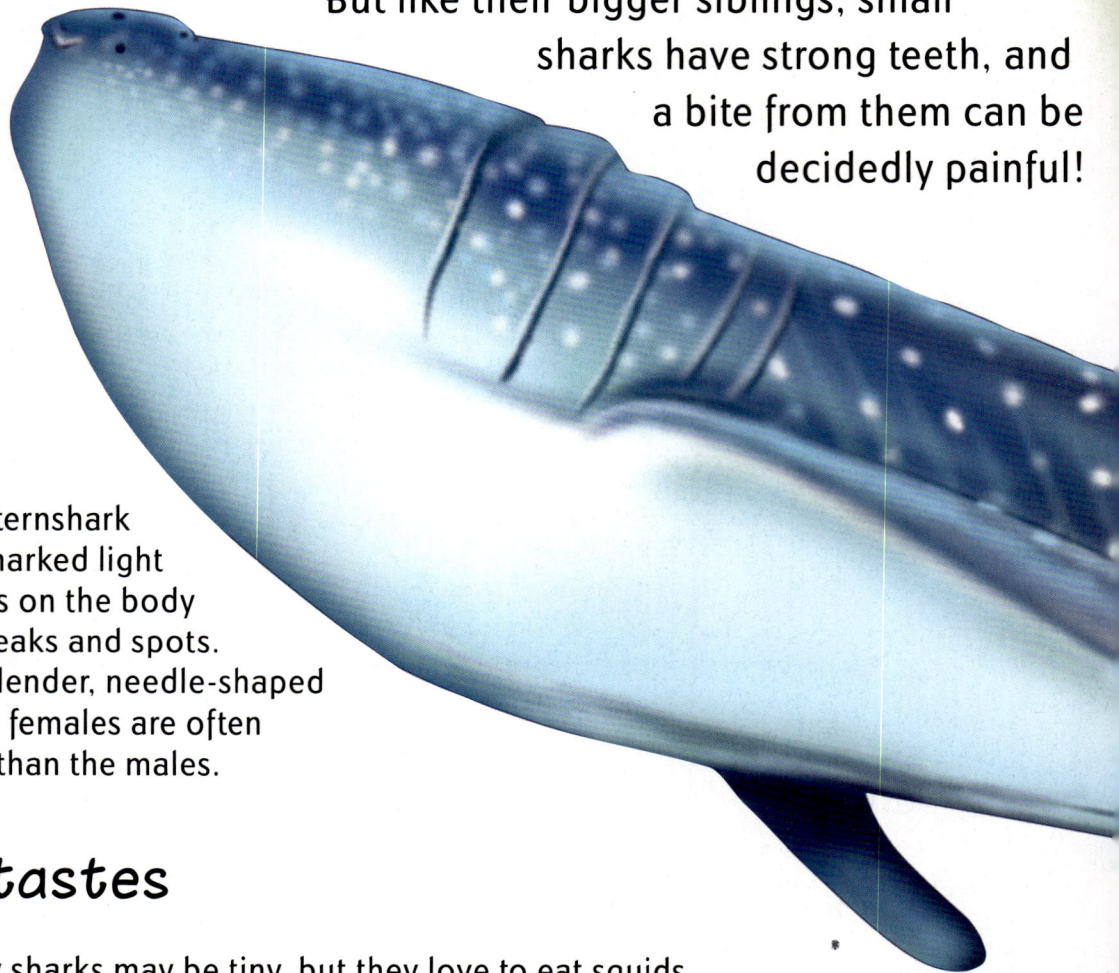

Marked bodies

The dwarf lanternshark has strongly marked light and dark areas on the body along with streaks and spots. The skin has slender, needle-shaped denticles. The females are often longer in size than the males.

Bigger tastes

Spined pygmy sharks may be tiny, but they love to eat squids, shrimps and mid-water fish. Their upper teeth are narrow and small, while the lower ones are large and knife-like.

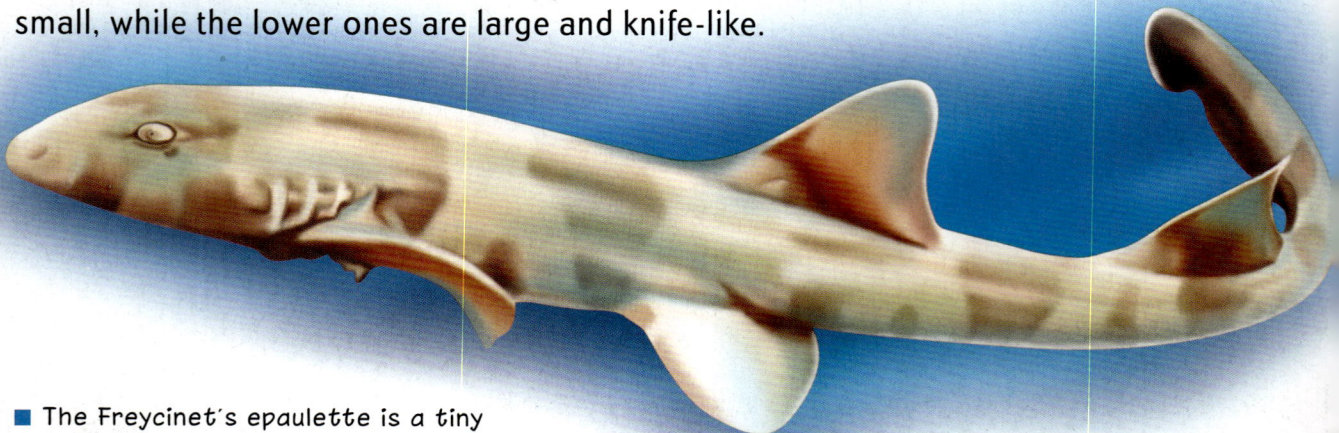

■ The Freycinet's epaulette is a tiny shark found in the coral reefs of Papua New Guinea. It hides during the day and hunts at night

Tiny and glowing

Spined pygmy sharks are very sleek and have a bulb-like snout. They are dark grey to black in colour and have white-tipped fins. Their bellies actually glow in the dark. They live in deep waters and are rarely seen.

FACT FILE

The dwarf lanternshark is 15-20 cm (6-8 inches) long
The spined pygmy shark is 18-20 cm (7-8 inches) long
The Pygmy ribbontail catshark is 15-20 cm (6-8 inches) long
The spined pygmy is found at depths of 2,000 m (6,550 feet)

■ The pygmy ribbontail catshark lives on the muddy ocean floor, on slopes and outer shelves. It looks tiny compared to the huge whale shark

INTERESTING FACT!

Spined pygmy sharks are commonly found at the bottom of the ocean. However, these sharks are known to journey up to about 198 m (650 feet) at night to hunt in the mid-water zones.

Ribbons undersea

Pygmy ribbontail catsharks are dark brown in colour with blackish markings on the fins. They are found around Tanzania, India, Vietnam and the Philippines. The small shark feeds on small bony fish and crustaceans.

The Great White Shark

Infamous for its appearance in the movie *Jaws* as a bloodthirsty man-eater, the great white shark is the largest predatory shark. The name *Jaws* was apt, given that this shark has as many as 3,000 razor-sharp teeth! It grows to over 4.5 m (14.7 feet) in length and weighs as much as 1,360 kg (3,000 pounds)! The great white is also known as the "white pointer" and "white death".

Where are they found?

Great white sharks live in temperate to warm waters. They are found across the world – from the coasts of America, the Gulf, Hawaii, South Africa and West Africa to Sandinavia, the Mediterranean Sea, Australia, New Zealand, Japan, and the eastern coastline of China and southern Russia.

Colour that helps

The great white is actually grey or bluish-grey in colour, with a white underbelly. Its colouring helps it to get close to its prey without being noticed. When seen from below, the white underbelly blends in with the bright reflection of the sky. Quite often, this shark attacks its victims by sneaking up quietly. The shark's greyish colour then helps it to blend in with the dark water.

■ Great white sharks are solitary creatures and prefer to swim alone. However, they have sometimes been sighted in pairs

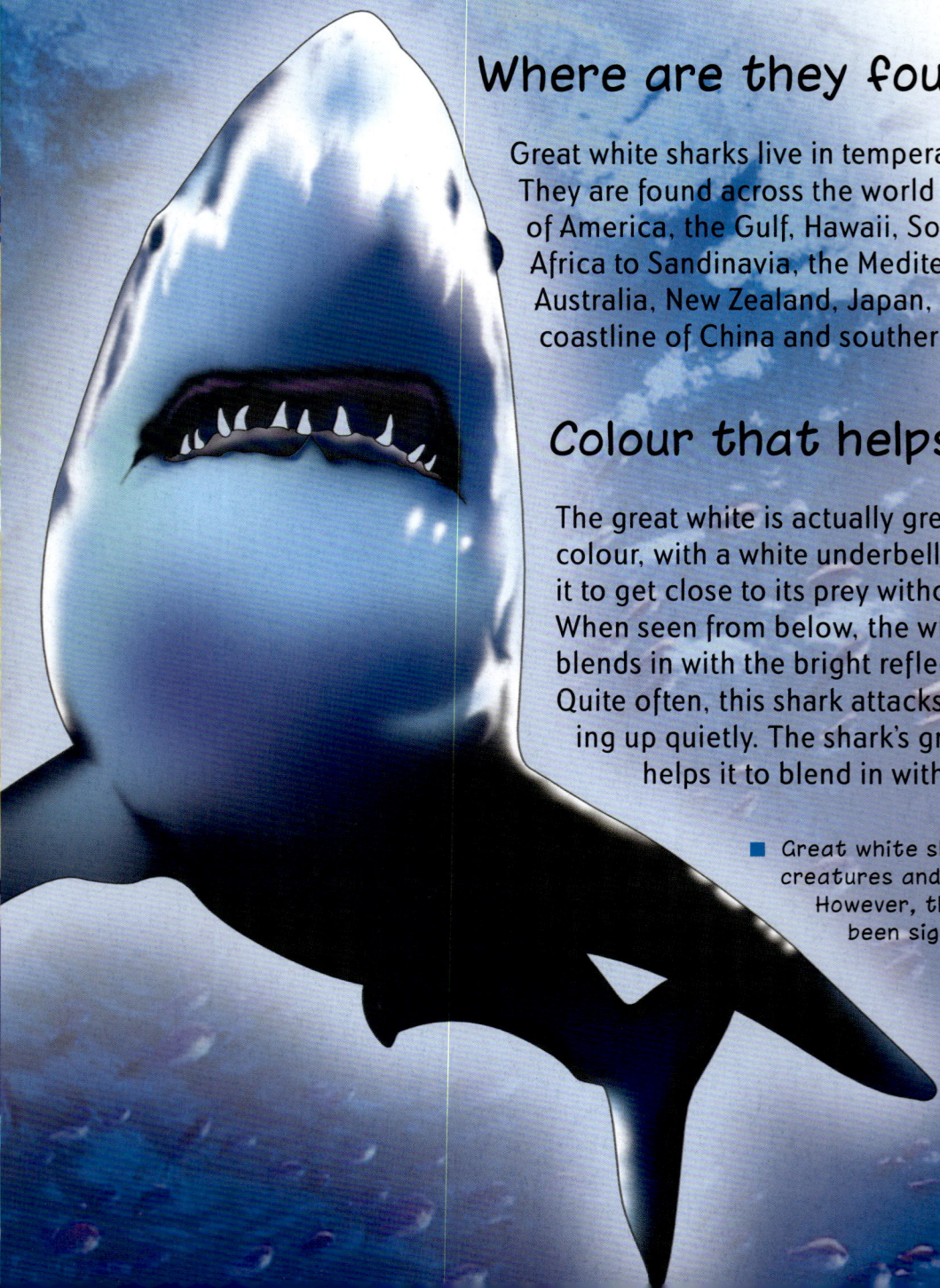

Fierce bite

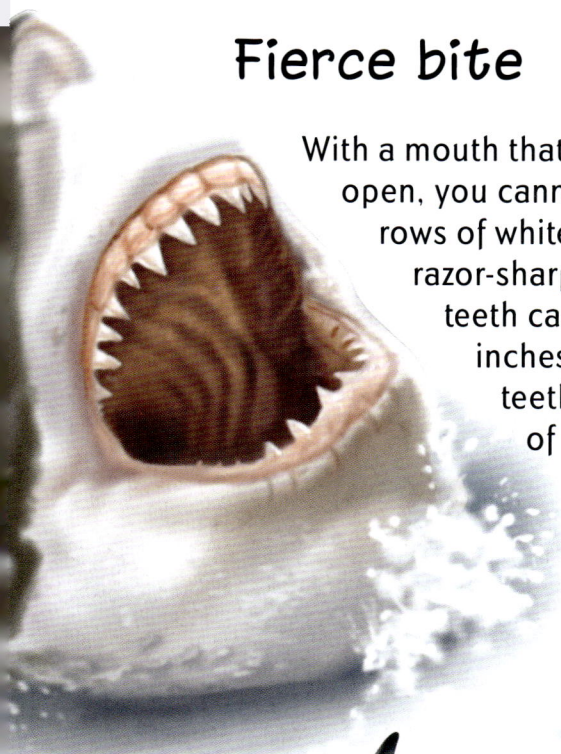

With a mouth that is most often open, you cannot miss the rows of white, triangle-shaped, razor-sharp teeth. The shark's teeth can grow up to 7.5 cm (3 inches) long. Old or broken teeth are replaced by a row of new teeth.

HABITAT

FACT FILE

Average length
3.6-4.9 m (12-16 feet)
Can grow up to
6.8 m (22.3 feet)
Can be as heavy as
3,312 kg (7,302 pounds)
Number of babies
2-14 pups
Shark attack
30-50 attacks per year
Fatal attacks
10-15 deaths every year
Can swim as deep as
250 m (775 feet)

INTERESTING FACT!

Great white sharks are ovoviviparous. The eggs of the great white remain inside the body of the female shark until they hatch. The female then gives birth to live young ones.

■ Great white sharks often jump out of the water while chasing seals. This is called breaching

What do they eat?

■ Great whites are known to attack pelicans, but they prefer to eat seals

Great whites eat dolphins, sea lions, seals, big bony fish and even penguins. Though they have earned a reputation for being man-eaters, they do not usually attack humans. These sharks are also scavengers, as they eat dead animals that float in water.

The great white first attacks its victim, injures it and then moves away. It approaches it later, when the pain and bleeding has weakened it. The shark does not chew its food, but rips the prey into mouth-sized pieces before swallowing them. After a good meal, the shark can do without another one for over a month!

Tiger Sharks and Bull Sharks

Many sharks, like the tiger and bull sharks, are named after land animals. The tiger shark has dark stripes on its back, similar to the big cat. But as the shark grows older, the stripes often fade away. The bull shark gets its name from its flat, wide and short snout, which resembles that of a bull.

■ Tiger sharks have good eyesight, which is aided by a special gill slit called a spiracle. Located behind the eye, this slit provides oxygen directly to the eyes and the brain

Tough tigers

The tiger shark has a very large mouth with powerful jaws. The triangular teeth of these sharks have saw-like edges that can slice through many objects. The tiger shark is not a very fast swimmer and often hunts at night.

Junk eaters

Tiger sharks love food and will eat almost anything. Biologists have found alarm clocks, tin cans, deer antlers and even shoes in the stomach of dead tiger sharks! Tiger sharks also feed on other sharks, fish, turtles and crabs.

■ Tiger sharks often prey on albatross chicks, which fall into the ocean while learning to fly

Bull sharks

The bull shark lives near coastal areas. It is also commonly found in rivers and freshwater lakes. Bull sharks eat fish, other sharks, turtles, birds and dolphins. Interestingly, adult female bull sharks are longer in size than male bull sharks.

FACT FILE

Tiger sharks are as long as 6 m (20 feet)
Bull sharks measure up to 3.5 m (11.5 feet)
Tiger sharks can live up to 30-40 years
Bull sharks can live up to 14 years
Tiger sharks swim at 3.9 km/h (2.4 mph)

Danger zone

It is dangerous to go near bull and tiger sharks, as they are known to be man-eaters. Tiger sharks are the second-most threatening species to humans, after the great white. Bull sharks rank third in this respect.

INTERESTING FACT!

Bull sharks travel from the upper Amazon River to the sea every season. They cover a distance of 3,700 km (2,300 miles) during this journey.

■ Bull sharks hardly have any predators. But there have been reports of crocodiles eating bull sharks

Pioneers of
New Zealand Wine

To Mike & Lynne
   With Very Best wishes
   for Xmas and The New Year
   From Marie 2002. xxx

Pioneers of
New Zealand Wine

Dick Scott

Photographs by Marti Friedlander

REED ◆ SOUTHERN CROSS

AUCKLAND

FRONT JACKET: Antonio Zame, Capri Vineyards, Gisborne. (Marti Friedlander)

BACK JACKET PAINTING: Graham Percy.

ENDPAPERS: French brothers bring in the vintage, Meeanee Mission, Hawkes Bay. (Courtesy Mission Vineyards)

DISPLAY PHOTOS FOR CHAPTERS THREE, FOUR, FIVE, SIX AND SEVEN: details from photos by Marti Friedlander.

Photos not credited to Marti Friedlander are from the author's collection, or as credited to other sources.

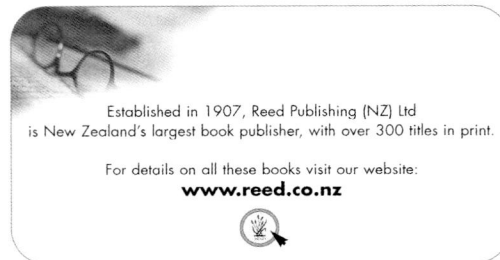

Established in 1907, Reed Publishing (NZ) Ltd
is New Zealand's largest book publisher, with over 300 titles in print.

For details on all these books visit our website:
www.reed.co.nz

Published by Reed Books in conjunction with Southern Cross Books, Auckland.
Reed Books is a division of Reed Publishing (NZ) Ltd,
39 Rawene Rd, Birkenhead, Auckland.
Associated companies, branches and representatives throughout the world.

ISBN 0 7900 0832 7

Text © 1964, 2002 Dick Scott
The author asserts his moral rights in the work.

Photographs © 2002 Marti Friedlander

Designed by Graeme Leather
Cover designed by Serena Kearns

First published as *Winemakers of New Zealand* by Southern Cross Books, Auckland, 1964

This edition by Reed Books/Southern Cross Books, 2002

Printed in Singapore

To

Joseph Soler, Spain

Israel Wendel, France

Heinrich Breidecker, Germany

Bartholomew Steinmetz, Luxembourg

Assid Abraham Corban, Lebanon

Charles Levet, England

Romeo Bragato, Italy

John Vella, Dalmatia

and all pioneer winemakers who transplanted

the skills of the old world to New Zealand

CANTERBURY PUNCH, 1865

MARTI FRIEDLANDER

Contents

Photographic sections

Preface
to the 2002 edition

Our world of wine has spun off into star-spangled orbit from the groundwork laid by the pioneers this book first celebrated in 1964. 'The last province to be added to the commonwealth of viticulture was New Zealand,' wrote Edward Hyams the following year in *Dionysus*, his authoritative social history of the wine vine. Two years later a paperback edition of *Winemakers of New Zealand* (the original title of this book), circulated to members of the newly formed Connoisseurs' Club, signalled that popular acceptance of wine was at last beginning.

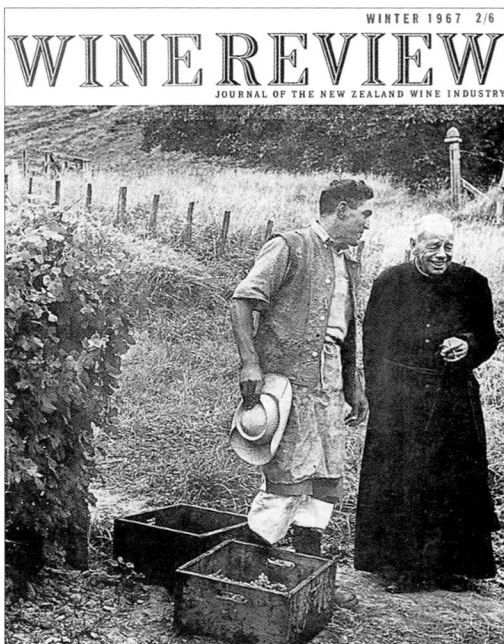

WINTER 1967 2/6
WINE REVIEW
JOURNAL OF THE NEW ZEALAND WINE INDUSTRY

The million-gallon output of that time has burgeoned to over 53 million litres a year. No longer forced to offer undeveloped palates 'Champagne', 'Chablis', 'Madeira', 'Port' and other Continental blends from the unexciting hybrid grapes in every vineyard, today's wine producers nurture classic varieties, produce fine wines with their own New Zealand personalities, and send 19 million litres ($200 million worth) each year to discerning markets around the world.

Travelling the vineyards as a photographer for *Wine Review*, the author's quarterly journal published 1964–78, Marti Friedlander captured the years of take-off with studies of the rugged characters who had weathered all manner of difficulties in their family enterprises, as well as the bold architects of expansion who introduced Gisborne and Marlborough to thousands of acres of vines along with multiple-armed spraying machines, robot-finger harvesting and all the other transformations that engineered an industrial revolution for wine manufacture. With empathy for her subjects and a rare camera eye, Marti Friedlander transports us back as witnesses to a significant period in our history.

Full credit is due to Peter Dowling as editor, and designers Sharon Whitaker and Graeme Leather, for marrying book and photographs in twenty-first century style.

Dick Scott

Dick Scott
April 2002

Acknowledgements

This is a book about the people who made the wine industry of New Zealand. They came from every wine country in Europe, stubborn, dedicated men, slightly odd in the eyes of their neighbours, who set themselves to clothe despised corners of the land in vines. Their names have not previously been celebrated — between James Busby's first efforts and twentieth-century winemaking, written history shows a totally blank page — and this account has depended for any colour it may have on the recollections of their descendants.

Among those who have assisted in establishing biographical details of nineteenth-century winemakers I am especially indebted to the Becroft, Levet and Lees families of North Auckland; F.J. Soler, Marton; and Christine Wendel, Auckland.

Valuable information has been obtained from Tom McDonald of Hawkes Bay who also made available the diary of S.F. Anderson, first winemaker at Greenmeadows; the Corban family whose records include copies of evidence to numerous parliamentary committees; Stephen Jelicich on early Dalmatian winemakers; and from Cecil Vidal and Brother Sylvester.

The editor of the *N.Z. Farmer*, John Cornwell, kindly allowed me to consult files of this journal dating from 1885; the Auckland Institute and Museum Library gave free use of its rich holdings from Busby's pamphlets to Romeo Bragato's reports; the Auckland University Library made available a geography thesis, *Viticulture and Winemaking in New Zealand*, by Warren Moran.

Tribute is due to Khaleel Corban, amateur photographer, whose collection of glass negatives, washed overnight in a creek and developed in the few hours between daylight work in the vineyard and night work in the winery, forms a unique part of the winemaking history that I have drawn upon to illustrate several sections of the book. I would also like to record appreciation of the generosity of Arend Bandsma and Robin Brandt who photographed with such care the medal (loaned by Moscow Yelas of Pleasant Valley Wines) that appears on the title page.

It is a pleasure to recall hospitality received at very many vineyards visited throughout Henderson and Hawkes Bay, and in designing the layout of text and illustrations for this book I am especially grateful for helpful criticism from my wife.

Measurements

For historical accuracy, imperial measures have been retained in many instances in this edition. Conversions are as follows:

MEASURES: 12 inches = 1 foot

3 feet = 1 yard = 0.9144 metres

1 chain = 66 feet = 20 metres

1 mile = 1.609 kilometres

1 acre = 0.405 hectares

1 gallon = 4.546 litres

WEIGHT: 16 ounces = 1 pound = 0.4536 kilograms

1 ton = 20 hundredweight = 1.016 tonnes

MONEY: 12 pence = 1 shilling

20 shillings = 1 pound = $2 (at 1967 value)

Ripe Clusters within Reach

Wine has always flowed in the land of promise lying buried in the English imagination. Somewhere in the first settlers' vision of new life in New Zealand were echoes of that great thirteenth-century verse, *The Land of Cockaygne*, which tells of a place better than paradise where

There are rivers gret and fine,
of oile, melk, honi and wine

Wines for Everyman

There were echoes, too, of More's *Utopia* which, two hundred years later, described an island of dainty meats, vineyards and grape wine where 'all things begin by little and little to wax pleasant. The air soft, temperate and gentle. The ground covered with green grass. Less wildness in the beasts.'

For nineteenth-century Englishmen the recurring theme seemed suddenly to take the shape of reality. Settlers bound for New Zealand could quicken their anticipation of a New Jerusalem with the tales of men who had been there, substantial men like James Busby, British Resident at the Bay of Islands, who convincingly held out the wines of Cockaygne and Utopia so that everyman might take his fill. Who could resist Busby's alternative to the gin mills of industrial Britain?

> One recommendation the settler's own wine will have is that it is of their own production — that they have planted the vines and pruned them — that their children, and families have gathered the grapes and 'brought home the vintage with shoutings' — that they have pressed them, and watched the fermentation of the juice — and that, in fact, the wine may be said in every respect to be their own.

Born in Edinburgh in 1801, the son of a Northumberland father and a Scottish mother enjoying the patronage of noble families, Busby spent several years as a young man living in the wine districts of France. The enthusiasm of his first pamphlet in praise of colonial winemaking, written on the voyage out to Australia in 1823, was not dimmed by actual experience of primitive conditions when he arrived. Shielded from practical difficulties by government appointments he continued to write persuasively.

In the *Manual of Plain Directions for Planting and Cultivating Vineyards and for Making Wine in New South Wales*, 1830, reprinted in New Zealand in 1862, and in *Authentic Information Relative to New South Wales and New Zealand*, 1831, he was if anything more ardent an advocate of colonial possibilities than ever. Vines were few, he admitted:

> And yet the man who could sit under the shade of his own vine, with his wife and children about him and the ripe clusters hanging within their reach, in such a climate as this,

and not feel the highest enjoyment, is incapable of happiness and does not know what the word means.

Busby could see peasant harvest customs reborn in the colonies: '. . . if those who are fond of mirth, knew with what rejoicing and revelry, this joyous season is welcomed throughout the wine countries, they would plant a vineyard, for this end alone, that they might anticipate the coming vintage, and exult in the fruits of their labour when it should arrive' — a suggestion of vine-garlanded Australians and New Zealanders dancing to Bacchus that would have strangely stirred the roaring citizens of Sydney Town and the beach of Kororareka had they been given to reading Busby's or any other books of improvement.

Before settling in New Zealand in 1833, Busby returned to England, made a four-month tour of European vineyards and, at the expense of the British government, selected cuttings in great number from French and Spanish varieties for New South Wales. Many were planted at the Sydney Botanical Gardens, some at Busby's own Hunter River Valley vineyard and he took vines with him to the Bay of Islands.

Busby's great optimism for the future of Australasian winemaking was shared by George Suttor, a fellow colonist. Planting his first successful vineyard at Parramatta in 1835 and claiming knowledge of New Zealand through a visit made to the Bay of Islands by his son in 1836–38 ('and grapes were there in abundance') Suttor could see the vine bringing social benefits under the Southern Cross. In *The Culture of the Grape-vine and the Orange in Australia and New Zealand*, published in London in 1843, he declared that both countries were so favoured by nature that it was unnecessary to confine production to the staples of pioneer economy, corn and cattle:

> Instead of choice fruits and wines being rarities for the wealthy, they might speedily, with due attention, be made so to abound, as not only to be shared and enjoyed by the humblest, but to become staples for export to less favoured countries, and even to rival those to whom the colonists now look for supplies.

Suttor then reproduced an argument of Busby's that supporters of

James Busby, first winemaker.

New Zealand winemaking have since used — in substance, if not with such elegance of phrase — whenever the industry has come under attack from prohibitionists. Said Suttor:

> Moral and Political considerations also may be strongly urged as inducements to a more general and earnest endeavour to raise the fruit of the vine into the rank of a staple produce of those countries. Wine will become the native beverage and, as in France, will tend to confirm habits of sobriety in the population. It is the most pleasant and refreshing drink that man could enjoy in a warm climate; and when not too strong promotes his health. Those to whom a refreshing draught of pure water is repulsive, have now no choice between heavy malt liquor and ardent spirits. Thousands would turn away from these in disgust could they readily procure relief for their thirst in a draught of fine flavoured though weak wine.

A New Zealand Company propagandist, the Honourable Henry William Petrie, who had spent a year with the first settlers at Port Nicholson, did not allow Cook Strait weather to spoil the story. Many of the hundred vine cuttings he had taken from Sydney to plant there were flourishing, he reported in a booklet that had run to four editions by 1842: 'From the nature of the climate at Port Nicholson, there can be no doubt of the ultimate success of the vine . . .' One drawback, he admitted, was that the English knew nothing about vines. 'To cultivate them to any extent, we require French and German cultivators, to whom the most liberal encouragement should be given. The few French at Akaroa, on Bank's peninsula, have begun to make a business of cultivating the vine, and, I am told, with every prospect of success.'

Even more rosy was the future painted three years later by an English author who claimed New Zealand experience (four years in the text, five on the title page). In *Remarks on the Past and Present State of New Zealand*, Walter Brodie wrote in 1845:

> New Zealand in a few years will export much wine. The vine grows very luxuriantly, and the few hundred of Germans who have lately gone out, have turned their attention to the vine alone. At the Northern part of New Zealand all English fruits abound, and grow in great luxuriance. The missionaries

having been out there for thirty years, nearly all the English fruits may be obtained: Grapes, peaches, quinces, and figs may be found wherever there is, or has been a native settlement.

Brodie's other exports — including shark fins and salt fish to China, iron ore ('there are hills of iron sand enough to load all the ships in the world'), lead, silver, and an island of rock salt ('only known to two parties') — suggest an element of exaggeration in his account of single-crop vine-growing Germans. Yet two shiploads of German vignerons had landed at Nelson in 1843 and 1844, attracted by the glowing prospects for viticulture promised them by the New Zealand Company. There were 140 on the *St Pauli* and 200 on the *Skiold* and the *Nelson Examiner* welcomed them warmly: 'No emigrants are more valuable than the Germans and we hail the intended cultivation of the vine by them with unfeigned pleasure.' By the time Brodie's book appeared, however, most had already been disillusioned and had left for the infant vineyards of South Australia.

Unlike the unscrupulous company and some of the later promoters of viticulture in New Zealand, Brodie had at least been frank about his intentions: '. . . I trust that what I have said may be relied upon, and be the means of inducing some of the rich capitalists in this country to invest a portion of their money there — all we want is money.'

Kerikeri mission station, where wines were planted in 1819. The pointed tower at left has been erected for a Maori feast — and by this time (1835) no feast was complete without grapes.

RIPE CLUSTERS
WITHIN REACH

Mr Busby's Delicious Light White

In truth, by this time Busby had been growing wine grapes at the Bay of Islands for more than ten years and as early as 1819 Marsden had planted about a hundred vines at his mission station at Kerikeri. Despite some talk at first of a Maori propensity to dig up year-old vines in search of a root crop, their agricultural skill swiftly adapted to grape culture. Darwin noted that grapes were among the fruits flourishing under Maori care at the Bay of Islands mission gardens when he called in 1835 on his round-the-world voyage in the *Beagle* — an observation the New Zealand Company was quick to reprint for the encouragement of intending settlers — and listing crops favoured by the Maori, the trader, Joel Polack, wrote in 1838 that 'grapes are largely cultivated to the northward of the River Thames'.

But for Busby, no purple flood poured from bursting harvests. Only his salary as British Resident permitted him to follow his passion for viticulture. Three years after settling at Waitangi, in a letter to Australia dated 14 November 1836, he included this message for his brother: 'Tell John with my love that the vines were planted out under the most favourable circumstances, just after a soaking rain. I think the majority of them are likely to survive. The season has been extremely moist.' Then there is a hint of slow progress in the answer to a request for cuttings received from Adelaide in 1839. His Waitangi collection was 'exceedingly deficient' he wrote, and he arranged for vines to be sent to the enquirer from his old stocks in Sydney Botanical Gardens.

By 1840 he was enjoying results. Dumont d'Urville, who visited New Zealand that year as commander of the *Astrolabe*, noted in his journal (in Olive Wright's translation):

As I was going over Mr Busby's estate, I noticed a trellis on which several flourishing vines were growing. I asked Mr Flint if the vines produced any grapes in this climate and, contrary to what I had been told in Korora Reka, I heard to my surprise that there had already been attempts to make wine from New Zealand grapes. On reaching his house Mr Flint offered me a glass of port. I refused it, but with great pleasure I agreed to taste the product of the vineyard that I had just seen. I was given a light white wine, very sparkling, and delicious to taste, which I enjoyed very much. Judging from this sample, I have no doubt that vines will be grown extensively all over the sandy hills of these islands, and very soon New Zealand wine may be exported to English possessions in India.

Two years after d'Urville's visit Busby reported bad news to his brother-in-law, W.D. Kelman, who had taken over his vineyard in the Hunter River Valley: 'My vines are open to the ravages of horses, sheep, cattle, and pigs. The leaves are nipped off as soon as they come out. The trees in the garden . . . are also broken down and destroyed.'

Before long the vineyard suffered even more rough-shod invasion; British troops stationed at Waitangi completed its destruction. A grand-daughter of James Busby, Agnes Busby of Tokomaru Bay, recalled this family history in a note to Eric Ramsden published in the *Journal of the Royal Australian Historical Society*, October 1940:

> I have always been told that the vineyard was planted in front of the house between the dwelling and where the flagstaff now stands, and that it was destroyed by the soldiers camped there during Heke's war in 1845. When I remember Waitangi first the vines were in a glass-house at the right-hand side of the house. How long they had been there I do not know: at that time there were none growing outside.

Despite his difficulties Busby had made wine — and in sufficient quantity, according to Ramsden, to sell to the military in 1846. Called the wine industry's 'Australian Prophet', Busby might also be fairly named its New Zealand pioneer.

Busby's were distinctively frontier problems. Another grape-grower, William Powditch, who settled at the Bay of Islands before Busby, was already facing more commonplace difficulties. Powditch had moved forty-eight kilometres north to Whangaroa Harbour where he bought over 4000 acres (1620 hectares) between 1835 and 1839 and from there in July 1841 he sent seventy grape cuttings to Gilbert Mair at the Bay of Islands in case he 'should not get any from Mr Busby'. In a covering letter (still clearly readable) giving exhaustive instructions as to planting, cultivation and pruning he gave this advice:

The winds are so strong and frequent it is necessary to adopt the Cape plan to keep them as low as possible. Also to give them as much sun as possible — now the nearer the ground the greater the heat. Now I have before told you to prepare hedges. They must be very thick, at least 4 feet through and 9 or 10 feet high. Your vineyard should be divided (if not very much sheltered) into half acres or less and the hedges run as to front the N.W. — that is westerly in preference to easterly.

After further instructions he went on:

When all the fruit is fully formed and not less than the size of a small pea . . . thin out the leaves and expose the fruits as much as possible to the sun. You will now have the fruits as much as possible to the sun. You will now have to contend with the rats — for whom you must keep cats — and keep your fruit off the ground and also chip out the weeds frequently keeping the stem and root clear, clean and dry. Use always a hoe — the spade will go too deep and injure the roots. The kingfisher with his large bill will now dart at the fruits and destroy with one blow more than he can eat in a day — pepper the rascals well with small shot from daylight till dark.

As a former commander of the British warship *Royal George*, William Powditch was a worthy first recruit in the grapegrowers' battle of the birds.

Some Bush Brews

Captain Powditch moved to Auckland in the forties and became speaker in the provincial parliament. James Busby, who also entered politics, turned his pamphleteering energies from wine promotion to arguing the rights of his own land claims. After the spread of oidium, the powdery mildew from America which invaded European vines with disastrous results at mid-century — and Busby corresponded with France on this subject in 1857 — most colonists were happy to leave the mysteries of viticulture to non-British arrivals or to gentlemen-settlers with leisure to dabble with diseases in grape arbour or conservatory.

Writing in the *New Zealand Magazine* in 1862, David Hay, an Auckland nurseryman, lamented the neglect of viticulture, especially when it had been proved that good wine could be made in New Zealand, 'wine vastly superior to much of the unwholesome imported mixtures'. Echoing a thirty-two-year-old Busby pamphlet (reprinted at this time by David McIndoe in his *New Zealand Grape Vine Manual*), Hay wrote:

> If this branch of horticulture were better attended to in this colony it would be found a paying as well as pleasing occupation, a branch of the industry of quite a poetical character, and as being honourably mentioned in Scripture and by the ancients as a source of happiness. Let us then see every settler sitting under his vine . . . that he and his children may eat of the grapes and drink of his own sparkling wine.

Understandably immune to poetical considerations, the settlers continued to plump for the domestic wines they were accustomed to making in Britain. Plum wine, gooseberry wine, parsnip wine — the fruits and vegetables of most orchards and gardens were made to yield a variety of fermented beverages right up to the 'British Champagne' as an early Nelson directory described the product of its rhubarb wine recipe.

Apple cider was also popular in pioneer kitchens. Commercial cider-makers produced 'Sparkling Champagne Cider' in tens of thousands of gallons, one early manufacturer exhibiting testimonials to its excellence from bishops in Christchurch and Auckland and an archbishop in Brisbane. And perry, too, the product of pears, was made in quantity for home use and commercially to cheer waggoners and miners — and bishops — on their rounds.

Some colonists turned to the Maori for inspiration in finding the ingredients for a brew. From their encyclopaedic knowledge of plant life the Maori had learned to make a refreshing drink out of the fruit of a New Zealand species of *Coriaria*, the highly poisonous shrub tutu. The settlers contrived to convert this into what has been variously described as 'a highly suspicious wine' and a wine 'much esteemed for its flavour and richness'. In *Handbook of the New Zealand Flora*, 1867, Dr J.D. Hooker remarks: 'The juice is purple and affords a grateful beverage to the natives; and a wine, like elderberry wine, has been made from it. The seeds alone are said by some (the whole plant by others) to produce convulsions, delirium and death . . .'[1]

The best account of European use of tutu wine has been given by the Reverend J.W. Stack, who encountered a sample while touring South Island back country with Bishop Harper in 1859. Reaching a remote Canterbury station after a day in the saddle they were greeted by 'the lady of the house', a home winemaker delighted to hear Stack say that northern Maori made a 'wholesome beverage' from tutu juice. She was pleased, he relates, that at last someone had appeared 'who would appreciate what her nephews persisted in calling her "poisonous wine" but of which unknown to themselves they were constantly partaking in her cookeries. She at once produced a bottle and some wine glasses . . .' Both clergymen accepted a drink.

Stack gives a magnificent sequel:

Fortunately, neither of us did more than taste it. I was seated at the time on a high form without back or arm-rests, and beside me sat a chatty old gentleman, who was trying to make the best of the opportunity he rarely now got of having a listener from outside his home circle. A few seconds after swallowing the wine I lost all sense of feeling in my extremities, and felt as if I could not much longer retain my seat on the bench, and must fall forward on my face. I could hear the old gentleman talking volubly, but could not follow what he was saying. A mist shrouded everything in the room. As the thought flashed through my mind that I was poisoned, I felt the keenest compunction for having misled the Bishop by my assurances regarding the harmlessness of tutu juice, and for having perhaps endangered his life. Would it not be

---

1. While authorities agree that the drink made by the Maori was non-intoxicating, around the world tutu has been put to startling use. *New Zealand Medicinal Plants* by S.G. Brooker and R.C. Cooper lists a dozen Maori concoctions from the plant, ranging from a root preparation for neuralgia, rheumatism and eyestrain, an infusion of leaves for dysentery, a poultice of young shoots for bruises and broken bones to a mixture of juice from the pith for treating insanity. The *Coriaria ruscifolia* of Chile, almost identical with New Zealand tutu, was used in witchcraft, and in Mexico the drug tlolocoptetl is extracted from another close relative. Tutu's lethal ingredient tutin, first isolated by New Zealand scientists in 1901, is chemically similar to the poison of the European *Coriaria myrtifolia* which has been used as a stimulant and has been suggested for use in modern anti-shock therapy. Did no tohunga ever stumble on strange side-effects from this 'grateful beverage'?

BATTENS

MASHING TUB

STAGE

BUCKET

SPARE BATONS.

An ingenious wine-press recommended to early settlers by Brett's *Colonists' Guide*.

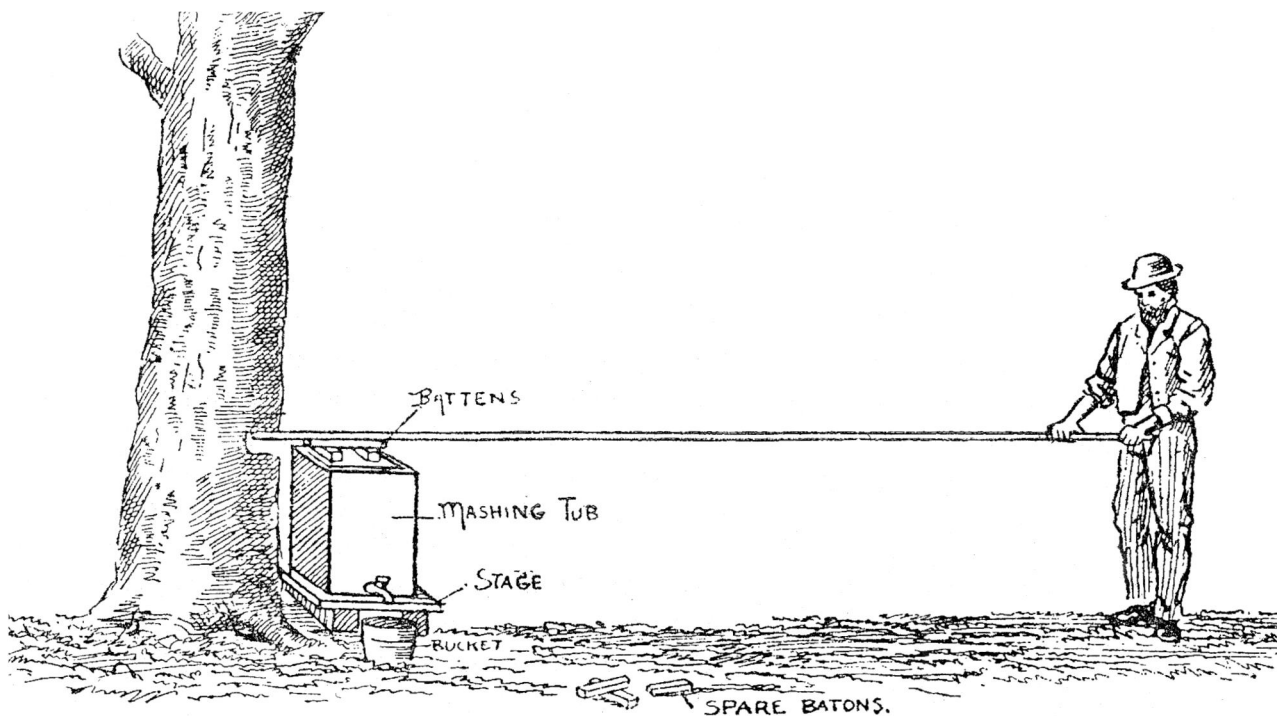

better to call out for an emetic before I lost consciousness, but what a ridiculous ending that would be to my praise of tutu wine? While I was making up my mind what to do, a tingling sensation in my extremities, and the vanishing of the mist from the room convinced me that the danger was all over. And with a sense of relief I turned to answer some question put to me by the old gentleman at my side. At the same time I looked anxiously at the Bishop, who was leaning back in his chair with a very serious expression on his face. Presently, he looked up and remarked: 'How very strong it is!' The subject of tutu wine was not referred to again by either of us till we were out of the house, when we compared notes about our sensations after tasting it, and we both agreed that it was not a beverage we could recommend for general use.

Perhaps domestic winemakers consoled themselves by comparing their product with imported wines. As an informed letter to the *Otago Daily Times* pointed out in 1870, the merchants regularly doctored their drinks, among other things making blackcurrant wine into sweet port. And:

. . . they add various substances to give flavour and warmth, qualities which drinkers appreciate. The consequence is

increased thirst, which, if yielded to, excites the passions, ending in a heavy sleep, followed by a terrible feeling of lassitude and horror, which is partially removed by a 'hair of the dog that bit them'.

Liquor refused admission to Melbourne 'had been received and sold at Port Chalmers', the writer said, and called for the appointment of a government analyst as in Victoria.

An analyst was engaged and samples of wine taken direct from bond in 1874 and 1875 were given these descriptions: 'Harsh flavour, feebly sour, much sediment and tartar'; 'decidedly acid to the taste and unpleasant, colour dark for sherry and turbid'; 'taste and smell of burnt sugar'. Three of four ports tested 'gave the reaction of elderberry wine', the other (from Australia) tasted new, 'being very harsh and astringent' and a group of sherries were 'clearly made up of brandy and caramel with flavouring matters'.

The reports cheerfully found none to be actually 'noxious'. This was an heroic age when the most desperate mixtures were good enough for colonial throats.

French Peasants and Priests

Thirty French peasants, some shirtless, some even without trousers, landed in New Zealand in 1840 carrying bundles of grape-vine cuttings, a few seeds and some fruit trees. With hand tools they confronted a rain forest, a tangle of trunks and undergrowth running to the sea from all the hills ringing Akaroa Harbour, and this was

Early Akaroa

the site for the new life promised by their sponsors, the Nanto-Bordelaise Company.

One of the thirty men, Emery de Malmanche from Rochefort in the Charente wine district, stood with his wife and children on the daunting shore and swore a great oath that his beard would go untrimmed until he saw France again — a resolution that took his whiskers below his waist, for the man-o-war *Aube* stood at anchor with the company's emigrant ship *Comte de Paris* to discourage such thoughts and sixteen years passed before he could make the voyage home.

Most of the settlers were from wine districts, uprooted from their homes by deep agricultural depression. Typical was the experience of Jean Pierre Eteveneaux, a vigneron from Jura. Three lean vintages in succession had driven him with his family to the seaport of Rochefort in search of a passage to Martinique. They arrived after their ship had gone, a newspaper advertisement announcing a settlement in 'Nouvelle-Zélande' caught their eye and with others in like plight they were driven to trust their fortunes to a land speculation company that offered free rations and free land on an island guaranteed to be under French sovereignty at the far side of the globe.

Akaroa sketched in April 1840
by Louis Le Breton.

The appearance of their new home was only the settlers' first disillusionment. That Christmas they marched in a body on the French naval commander, Captain Lavaud, to protest at 'the enormous prices of provisions charged to them' at the company store and Lavaud, a just man who had been appalled at the half-naked appearance of the emigrants when they first landed, sympathetically passed on their complaint. 'All this is not very good to animate the courage of the cultivators who already feel great disappointment at the sight of ungrateful soil upon which they are asked to work,' he reported to the minister of marine. But the captain of the *Aube* had no power to intervene in commercial matters. As the prospects that had beguiled the settlers to New Zealand evaporated one by one there was no alternative but to attempt to live from the land they had been given. In September 1841 Captain Lavaud wrote home:

> Every family has been able to work half an acre. They have sown some seeds and planted some potatoes, but the south-west winds are violent and cold, frequently accompanied by snow and hail, even at this time of the year . . . Some of the vines are raising our hopes, but will they resist the wind and the cold?

In November that year Governor Hobson suggested that the company abandon its claims to Banks Peninsula in exchange for land in the Far North. A grant would be made in proportion to its outlay of capital and at Kaitaia, he said in inducement, there was 'an abundance of fine land with an undulating surface, well adapted for vineyards'. But the company preferred to hold to its bargain of 30,000 acres (12,150 hectares) 'purchased' from some Maori (not the rightful owners) for waxed hats, clay pipes, casks of wine and similar trade goods to the value of 6000 francs (then about £240).

The settlers struggled on. With peasant tenacity they cleared their holdings to the five-acre maximum allowed by the company. It was harsh, subsistence-level farming but even subsistence could not be contemplated without grape-vines. The cuttings took root in the clearings, the vines flourished in bush soil, grapes were harvested and wine was made. Wine even helped for a time to preserve a cheerful peasant custom. On the feast days of the saints after whom the children had been named all the settlers would meet at the celebrating family's house; the wine jug passed, the latest vintage was savoured, someone would bring out a fiddle and there would be music and dancing. Every family in turn entertained the whole settlement in this way.

And beyond the needs of winemaking there was a surplus of grapes to sell visiting countrymen, French whalers starved for fresh fruit after months at sea. But Akaroa could not remain a fossil fragment of old France. The New Zealand Company and then a sequence of Native Land Purchase Commissioners took over the Nanto-Bordelaise Company's task of wresting Banks Peninsula from the Maori. British settlers occupied large tracts of land and the vineyards and the cottages established, in Pember Reeves' phrase, 'in a fashion having some pathetic reminiscence of rural France', were swamped by an alien culture.

When Romeo Bragato — an Italian viticulturist working for the government of Victoria in Australia — visited Akaroa in 1895, the oldest French settler, François Le Lievre, presented him with ripe grapes of the Chasselas, la Folle and Muscat-Frontignac varieties. They were pronounced 'all of very fine flavour' but Bragato lamented that the pioneers had 'failed to communicate to their offspring even a small percentage of that enthusiasm over the cultivation of the vine which they were in such a large measure possessed of.'

The vineyards that 'had been to their forbears as a bit of the fatherland' had all disappeared.

Bragato reported to the government that 'if capitalists could be induced to invest' and if the settlers 'would only enter upon the vine industry in a proper spirit and upon an extensive scale' they would produce wine similar to that of the Rhine and Moselle and Akaroa would become known as a vineyard of Christchurch and acquire worldwide fame. But in 1919, a quarter of a century later, when the poet Blanche Baughan described the Akaroa she loved, there had been no winemaking revival.

There was then nothing of the romantic French past

beyond the memory, and a faint, persisting, 'foreign' fragrance, very sweet to some of us. In the family names of many of the inhabitants we find it — Le Lievre, for instance, Libeau, Eteveneaux; in the names of the main streets — in Lavaud,

Jolie, Balgueri; in the tall poplars that vividly recall those long, white, poplar bordered roads of France; in the acacias, the tall old almonds, and the walnut groves. There are olives, too, and figs, lemons and orange-trees, in some of the Akaroa gardens; grapes ripen still on certain walls and banks . . .

Of winemaking there was no trace.

The Mission Plantings

The priests of the Society of Mary were to leave a more enduring impression on New Zealand winegrowing than the peasants of the Nanto-Bordelaise Company.

In 1836 Pope Gregory XVI declared the Pacific a field for missionary endeavour and appointed the French Marist Order to take charge of the work. In the five years from 1838 onwards, thirty-six French priests and lay brothers landed in New Zealand and along with the altar vessels in their luggage came carefully tended vine cuttings to maintain the supply of sacramental wine needed for the rites of their church. In addition, the Marists considered that the antipodes offered hardship enough without denying them wine for the table and also it was their policy — like Marsden's — to win support from the Maori by distributing such marvels as the grape. (In Fiji watered wine distributed to the sick was more popular than the brews of tribal priests until the Methodists outbid the field by bringing in a missionary doctor.)

Vines were planted at Hokianga, up the Whanganui River, in Poverty Bay and at Hawkes Bay — in whatever remote area the fathers gained a foothold, their progress was marked by patches of light green struggling against the bush and scrub on the edges of Maori settlements.

The work of planting was the special duty of the lay brothers, peasants who had taken vows of obedience, chastity and poverty and were ready to give a lifetime of unpaid labour to the church. Upon their efforts was ultimately established a permanent vineyard in Hawkes Bay.

In 1850 a large party of priests accompanied by Maori men-servants and lay brothers sailed from Auckland to establish missions in southern parts of the North Island. One group, comprising Father Lampila and Brothers Basil and Florentin, mistook the Poverty Bay coast for their Hawkes Bay destination and landed at

Brother Cyprian, winemaker at
Meeanee, 1871–99.

Turanganui, as Gisborne was then called. They settled, planted grape-vines, and not till the following year reached their intended landfall. And there, at Pakowhai, thirteen kilometres south of present-day Napier, a mission station was built. The vines then planted were the foundation of what is now New Zealand's oldest vineyard, not the oldest in terms of locality (the mission site was twice moved over the next half century) but the oldest with continuity of management.

Before being sent to fresh spiritual pastures on the upper Whanganui River at the end of 1852, Father Lampila revisited Poverty Bay. There, official church history records, 'he found the little vineyard that the brothers had planted bearing a small crop of well-ripened grapes, and, as wine for altar purposes was much needed, he spent some time in wine-making.' Perhaps the first mistaken landing and now the fate of Father Lampila's wine were portents of the misfortunes that later plagued the mission vineyards; when the priest sent a small barrelful by sea to Hawkes Bay the sailors broached the cask, drank the contents, and refilled it with salt water.

At Pakowhai, where Father Regnier had replaced Father Lampila, the brothers were growing crops, grinding flour on a hand-mill and running a store to trade with the Maori — those, that is, who owed no allegiance to William Colenso's Protestant mission already established in the district. The two missions' common interest in making wine (Colenso offered raspberry wine to his visitors) was not common ground enough to over-ride sectarian differences. Doctrinal dispute grafted on old tribal enmities was leading towards bloodshed by 1855 and, anticipating trouble, the proceeds of the brothers' trading store were used to buy an alternative site of 326 acres (132 hectares) at nearby Meeanee. Three years later, when the Catholic-supporting tribe was defeated and its chief killed, the mission buildings were shifted in sections by bullock waggon to their new headquarters. Farming, milling, storekeeping and re-establishing at Meeanee left little time for tending grapes or wine-press. In 1871 the vines and winemaking received their first serious attention with the arrival of Brother Cyprian who, as Lawrence Huchet of the Loire, had learned the business of a vigneron from his father.

A delegation sent to New Zealand in 1879 by the tenant farmers of Lincolnshire to investigate emigration prospects almost certainly

Andrew Tod, a Scottish winemaker with export ambitions, depended on Maori-grown grapes brought downriver by the canoe-load. The *Dundee Advertiser* noted in 1875 that his wines 'of excellent quality had improved rather than deteriorated in bouquet by the long voyage'. In 1877 Wellington's *Evening Argus* reported that 'judges of wine unhesitatingly declare it to be superior to those of Australian manufacture'.

A grape-laden Maori street-seller displays his wares for an Auckland 'photographic saloon'.

were referring to Brother Cyprian's work at the mission vineyards when they reported that they had seen grapes growing outdoors in Hawkes Bay. They wrote: 'Near Tutai Kuri we saw a garden in which a very large quantity of grapes were growing beautifully in the open air. The vines were arranged on trellis-work and comprised a great many varieties, all apparently growing nearly equally well.'

The area under grapes remained small but Brother Cyprian made good wine. At the suggestion of the French consul in New Zealand, Count Alexandre d'Abbans, samples of the mission vintages of 1885–88 were sent to the Paris Exhibition of 1892. A silver medal was won, and praise from French connoisseurs. When Romeo Bragato, the Victorian Government expert, visited the Meeanee Mission in 1895 he found the wine from its three-acre vineyard 'most exquisite', reminding him of 'the liqueur wine produced on the Greek Archipelago Islands'.

Overshadowing success was a constant threat of flooding from the adjoining Tutaekuri and Ngaruroro rivers. In the winter of 1897 both rivers simultaneously broke their banks and inundated the

Tom McDonald sledges out grapes in 1929, two years after taking over the Steinmetz vineyard planted at Greenmeadows, Hawkes Bay, over thirty years before.

plains of lower Meeanee. The vines were silted up, the cellar was afloat and floodwaters invaded the church. It was decided to move once more, this time to higher ground, and 600 acres (243 hectares) were purchased on the hill slopes of Greenmeadows from the estate of Hawkes Bay landowner Henry Tiffen.

At first only the Meeanee winemaking enterprise was moved but after a further flood reached the feet of a new statue of the Virgin Mary the day it was blessed by Archbishop Redwood, all mission activities were transferred to Greenmeadows. The brothers planted nine acres of vines, brick cellars were built and so monastic routine, still punctuated by occasional calamity,[1] continued into the twentieth century.

Indirectly, the mission had a wider influence on the industry. A brother, Bartholomew Steinmetz of Luxembourg, who had left the mission in 1897 to start his own vineyard (and to marry) planted five acres in the same district and for over thirty years successfully made wine. In 1927 a young man, Tom McDonald, who worked for Steinmetz, took over his vineyard and began McDonald Wines.

1. In 1929 an unexplained fire broke out in the wine vaults, large stocks of wine poured out from burning vats and severe damage was done to the cellars; the Hawkes Bay earthquake of 1931 tore 1000-gallon tuns from their base and hurled them to the floor (two priests and seven students died in a nearby chapel); in 1954 weed hormones sprayed by air on the mission farm drifted to the vineyard and destroyed a large part of it.

Joseph Soler's wine vessels: the glazed pottery barrel was one of
several made from local clay for his Wanganui wineshop, first licensed
in 1881.

(MARTI FRIEDLANDER)

Father and son Charles and William Levet at the door of their rough-sawn kauri winery, Lord Glasgow Vineyards, established on the Kaipara in 1863.

OPPOSITE
The Levets' wine-press, grape crusher and hand-blown bottle, recovered in 1964 by the author and his daughter and deposited in the Auckland Museum.

(GRAHAM MCKECHNIE, AUCKLAND STAR)

The whole family gathers to wash out barrels in readiness for a new vintage at Francis H.M. Ellis and Sons' winery at Golden Bay, Nelson. Vines were first planted at the foot of this harsh outcrop from Takaka's marble mountain in 1868. In 1895 (about the time the photograph was taken) Romeo Bragato found the vineyard 'in a fine healthy and luxuriant condition'.

(TYREE)

OPPOSITE

Eileen Allen savours the last bottle from a case her uncle, Francis Ellis, gave as a wedding present sixty years before.

(MARTI FRIEDLANDER)

CHRISTOPHER FRANK,

HARDY STREET,

NELSON.

CELEBRATED VINE GROWER

AND

WINE MAKER.

Christopher Frank's advertisement appeared in *Lucas's Nelson Directory*, 1874.

Israel Wendel, a native of Alsace-Lorraine, planted his first vineyard in 1872 in what is now central Auckland's Greys Avenue. The Colonial Wine and Champagne Factory moved to Symonds Street in the 1880s when Wendel's Wine Bodega also opened in Karangahape Road. His daughter Brunetta (below) carried on winemaking and ran the wine shop after her father died in 1895.

OPPOSITE

Wendel's cellarman measures the progress of his wines with the care that won both national and international medals.

(HENRY WINKELMANN)

The Posinkovich vineyard at Herekino in the Far North, 1903.
(NORTHWOOD)

OPPOSITE
Kohukohu, wine capital of the north, about 1900. Robert Lester's
five-acre terraced vineyard and orchard above the timber port was
one of at least four commercial vineyards in the region.

OPPOSITE BELOW
Awaiting a visit from the governor, Lord Ranfurly, in 1899, father and
son winemakers Heinrich and Johann Breidecker stand among their
low-growing vines planted at Kokukohu fifteen years earlier.

Pickers on William Beetham's Lansdowne Vineyard, Masterton, muster in their Sunday best for a *New Zealand Graphic* photographer in 1897. They were paid two shillings for a nine-hour day; the grapes were trodden by bare feet.

(*NEW ZEALAND GRAPHIC*)

OPPOSITE

Heralded in the 1890s as 'an example to the country', W.H. Jackman's vineyard at Whakapirau, Kaipara Harbour, produced fine wines from six acres of classic grapes.

(WASH DRAWING FROM THE *NEW ZEALAND GRAPHIC*, BY E.B. VAUGHAN, 1900)

One small back bends double in 1896 to shovel grapes on the elevator — virtually the only manual work in the winery at Henry Tiffen's model Greenmeadows Vineyard.

(*NEW ZEALAND FARMER*)

W. Heathcote Jackman, pictured with son Guy, learned winemaking from his library of translated French works. Growing classic grapes in the nineteenth century, he was decades ahead of his time.

Joseph Balich, a Dalmatian deserter from the Austrian Army, and his family beside the van which travelled door-to-door offering invalid port from his Golden Sunset Vineyards (established in 1912). Advertising at the time always stressed the 'medicinal' factor to counteract prohibition propaganda.

Dudley Russell dispatches a bumper order — one case — from the vineyard he began planting as a nineteen-year-old in 1932. With total capital of £100, he contoured and landscaped twenty-four acres (ten hectares) of abandoned land up the Henderson Valley to create Western Vineyards as the industry's showplace.

Assid Abraham Corban on arrival in New Zealand in 1892.

First Commercial Successes

A middle-aged Englishman and his fourteen-year-old son who began clearing and stumping kauri bush on a tidal arm of Kaipara Harbour in 1863 were New Zealand's first winemakers to earn a living exclusively from their own vineyard. The father, Charles Levet, a coppersmith from Ely, Cambridgeshire, had brought his family out on the *Hanover*, one of

A Coppersmith at Kaipara

the Albertland settlement ships, with no other resources but the strength of his determination to make wine.[1]

He took up land at Wellsford, thirteen kilometres by water from Port Albert. The country was hilly and thickly timbered, the soil stiff and hard, and Levet and his son William carved out their vineyard by back-breaking labour. They planted vines against manuka stakes set two, three or four feet high according to the slope of the ground, and from the top of these stakes rough manuka rods were run towards the face of the hill. The vines were trailed along these horizontals, the bunches of fruit hanging almost to the ground at the up-slope end. Seven acres were planted, tied to this rude trellis work and thereafter cultivated by hand. And to keep off the cold south-westerlies that sometimes blasted across the harbour, long lines of high paling fences were built across the vineyard.

The Levets built their own pit-sawn, vertical-boarded wine house and from kauri planks fashioned their own wine-press. The cellar was simply a lean-to running on the two cool sides of their first bush cottage.

Father and son struggled for years to establish their vines, discover the most suitable varieties, learn how to best prune them, and master the winemaking process. They lived in the meantime by floating out kauri logs for sale, by mill work and by splitting kauri shingles for the roofs of Auckland.

Even for settlers farming on orthodox lines, the first years at Albertland were hard enough. Local history is full of tales of how the pioneers made great cross-country journeys on foot, a bag of flour across the shoulders, to bring food to half-starved families: the non-arrival of coastal supply boats, the only communication with the outside world, sometimes reduced the people to eating rats and boiled sow thistle.

The Levets faced manmade difficulties as well. Though greatly given to dancing — no function ended without a dance, including meetings of the Total Abstinence Society — the Albertlanders were stern nonconformists who permitted no hotels in their district and at this time the Licensing Act made no provision for the sale of wine

PATRONISED BY
THEIR EXCEL-
LENCIES

SIR WILLIAM JER-
VOIS, K.C.B., AND
LORD GLASGOW.

THE VINEYARD, WELLSFORD, KAIPARA, N.Z.

PURE   WINES.

ESTABLISHED 1863.

LORD GLASGOW
VINEYARDS,
WELLSFORD.

G. LEVET & SON'S
.. WINES ..
ARE STILL TO THE FRONT,

The Vineyards are the largest North of Auckland, whilst the stock and quality of their
Wines are not to be equalled for

Purity, Maturity and Soundness.

As an established Firm of
THIRTY-FIVE YEARS,
Our motto has been
QUALITY, NOT QUANTITY,

And on this head we have built our present
trade, which is impregnable to competition,

BOTH IN QUALITY AND PRICE.

Auckland Star advertisement, 1898.

1. In a letter to the author, a grandson, C.V. Levet of Te Hana, Wellsford, writes: 'I remember as a boy seeing a large book on viticulture and winemaking and I presume it was from the study of this that a coppersmith and his son became successful winemakers.'

other than by hotels. Seymour George, member for Rodney, took up their case in 1879 and two years after he had raised the matter in parliament the law was amended to allow vineyard sales and the licensing of wine shops.

Shops were permitted to open (in boroughs only) for the sale of local wine, cider and perry of a strength not exceeding twenty per cent proof spirit. These could be consumed on or off the premises.

The first licence was granted to Israel Wendel, a native of Alsace-Lorraine who had made wine in the cellars of his house in Symonds Street, Auckland, since the early seventies. He opened a wine bar in Karangahape Road and thereafter the Levets could row their barrels thirteen kilometres by tidal creek to Port Albert for shipment via Onehunga to the glittering shelves of Wendel's Wine Bodega, open for trade from six o'clock in the morning until ten at night.[2]

Less generously, the 1881 amendment provided that winemakers themselves could not sell from their vineyard except in quantities of two gallons or more for consumption off the premises.

This restriction had been opposed in the House by William Swanson, member for Newton, who asked why a traveller could not refresh himself with the product of vineyards he came upon in the countryside:

> If a man happened to live a little way out of town and kept cows he might supply travellers with butter, cheese, curds and cream, or milk; but if he happened to have a vineyard he could not sell a glass of his wine without the risk of finding himself on the wrong side of the gaol.

In a country reeling with drunkenness this was altogether too civilised a proposition and it was three-quarters of a century before the two-gallon limit was relaxed to allow bottle sales by winegrowers.

---

2. Wendel's house at 71 Symonds Street was still standing in 1964, occupied by a grand-daughter-in-law. Originally quarters for officers and men engaged in the New Zealand Wars, it was purchased from the government for £500 and the entire basement was converted into cellars. When Israel Wendel died in 1895 his daughter Brunetta continued winemaking and, as Mrs A. Trevethick, for many years operated the Karangahape Road winebar. It was subsequently transferred to 173 Karangahape Road (on the opposite side of the street) where Dominion Wines Ltd held the licence.

The Levets' wine was made mostly from Isabella grapes blended with a few Black Hamburghs, and from the white Sweetwater. Port, sherry, madeira and constantia were produced, all unfortified and matured in oak for five years. Sometimes a small quantity of peach and strawberry wine and cider was also made.

An early visitor commented that the Isabellas were free of the disagreeable musky flavour usually associated with that grape. Writing in the *Farmer* he said:

> We are almost ashamed to remember how many different barrels of wine we sampled in Mr Levet's hospitable cellar, but we can truthfully say that there may be a headache in a hogshead of it, there is no headache in as many glasses as any rational being would care to drink at one sitting.

Even teetotal Albertlanders must have been impressed with the cuckoo industry in their midst when eventually a stream of wine cases crossed the Port Albert wharves addressed to Government House, Auckland. The governor, Sir William Jervois, was a regular customer during his term of office (1883–89) and a successor, the Earl of Glasgow (1892–97), was pleased enough with its quality to visit the Levets and grant them the right to name their property the Lord Glasgow Vineyards. A vice-regal coat-of-arms thereafter graced their label but this was not recognition enough to prevent their achievements being forgotten. Bragato was not taken to visit the Levets when he toured New Zealand in 1895, the reports of the Agriculture Department ignored them, and no history praises their name.

Father and son died within two years of each other, William in 1905 when still in his fifties, Charles in 1907 at the age of eighty-five. No members of the family were old or experienced enough to carry on and cows were turned on the vines, the wine press was used for cheese-making, the casks were sold to a Henderson winemaker, Assid Corban, and the labours of more than forty years might never have been.[3]

Joseph Soler.

---

3. In 1964 the author retrieved the original wine-press in a state of decay from the ruins of an old shed on the vineyard site. The owner of the land, J.A. Brunton, had made fence battens from a heart totara vat, the timbers of which, when sawn down the middle after more than half a century, still produced a strong aroma of wine.

In 1866, three years after the Levets had begun pioneering on the Kaipara, José Solé, a Spanish winemaker from Tarragona, crossed from the colony of Victoria to look around New Zealand. In his wanderings his eye was testing soil and climate and replacing raw bush clearings with the orderly vineyards of his homeland, for somewhere in Australia or New Zealand he was determined to find ideal wine country. He decided — perhaps influenced by the old French mission plantings up the river — that Wanganui was that place.

The Spaniard returned to Victoria to buy vine cuttings, planted them on a two-and-a-half acre section in Wanganui township, and three years later was making wine.

Joseph Soler (as his name was anglicized) could see that Wanganui soil was too cold to grow bunches of grapes low to the ground as in rocky Spain and so he built fences four feet high and trained the vines along two evenly spaced wires. From the classic wine-grapes of France and Spain he gained yields of six tons to the acre, scorning for many years to add manure to the soil.

With his own harvest, and grapes bought by the canoe-load at two pence a pound from Whanganui River Maori, Soler made a wide range of wines including, until he became too busy, sparkling burgundy and hock. He earned a living growing small fruits and vegetables while the vines established and the wines matured and was content to wait seven or eight years before releasing each vintage for sale. Word soon passed as to the quality of his product and before long he was shipping to discerning buyers all over New Zealand. As a Masterton magistrate wrote in the eighties to a friend: 'I have just had a case of Soler's Wanganui wine sent to me; it is quite equal to the best Australian and is a credit to the colony — the constantia is specially excellent.'

At the Melbourne International Exhibition, 1880, Soler's wines took six prizes and at the London Colonial and Indian Exhibition, 1886, they were placed third in competition with entries from all colonies including South Africa. These were only some of his overseas awards.

By now Soler's yearly trip to Maori settlements up the Whanganui River was yielding fewer grapes at each harvest. Where once he had bought seven canoe-loads at one stopping place, at the Hiruharama (Jerusalem) mission station, now not even the offer of threepence a pound was producing results. Joined by a nephew

Soler's Wanganui Wine

Cover of Joseph Soler's wine-list, printed in green, gold and black about 1899.

from Spain, the twenty-two-year-old Anthony Vidal, Soler built two large glasshouses on his town property in Bell Street, using the — for the time — impressive amount of 14,000 square feet of glass. On sixty acres (twenty-four hectares) purchased at Westmere, a few kilometres north of Wanganui, he planted an additional five acres of vines.

One of the wine bars licensed by the Act of 1881 was located in Wanganui to retail his product and he was now selling 3500 gallons a year.

His example had encouraged Cresci Minocheri, an Italian from Florence, to plant a quarter-acre of wine grapes in the same street and in 1896 a Frenchman, Jean Provost, with a countryman named du Flou as manager, took over a fruit-preserving works at Aramoho to convert it to large-scale cider manufacturing and some winemaking.

'Mr Soler has wines for the connoisseur', the *Farmer* reported in 1897 in a lengthy interview, 'Successful Winemaking in Wanganui', but added, 'from a European point of view, not nine out of ten in the colonial community are good judges of wine . . .' A sternly practical conclusion was drawn: 'He has found out the kind of wine the colonial palate prefers, and, as a businessman, he makes that wine. He does not theorize about educating the public as to what they ought to drink; he simply manufactures what they want to drink . . .'

A later article spelt out the popular preference:

. . . it is the stronger-bodied kind that appear to have best hit the paying colonial taste. The natural uneducated British taste, when it calls for wine, craves something that is red and sweet and strong. Good wine of a lighter kind might be better for the average drinker, but the ascent to that better state of affairs seems long and slow. For our drinking as a beverage with our meals, these light wines are advisable and would well vary and displace the tyrannous, unvarying tea, tea, tea . . .

Soler's business policy paid. That year the *Cyclopaedia of New Zealand* could say that he was reaping his reward for years of hard work and good management, citing as evidence of prosperity the size and solidity of his eight-roomed house built grandly on then

CHAPMAN'S

NEW ZEALAND

GRAPE VINE MANUAL

OR

PLAIN DIRECTIONS
FOR

PLANTING AND CULTIVATING VINEYARDS
AND FOR

MAKING WINES

EDITED BY DAVID McINDOE,
Head Gardener to Thomas Russell, Esq., Glenside, and Pah Farm.

NEW ZEALAND:
Published by G. T. CHAPMAN, Bookseller & Stationer,
QUEEN STREET, AUCKLAND.

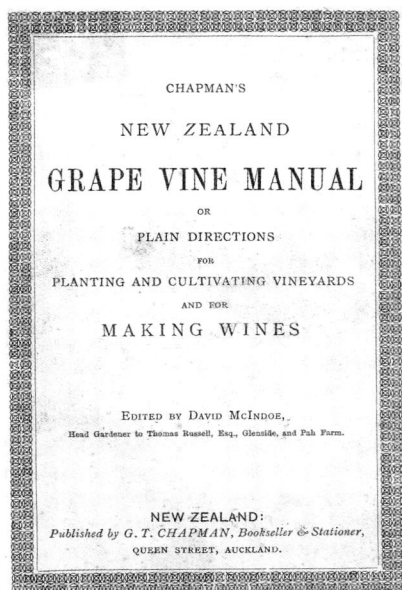

Only the Alexander Turnbull Library holds this rare 1875 textbook, which included 'correspondence and conversations on the subject with nearly all the most intelligent local gardeners and wine growers' and reprinted in full (42 pages) James Busby's wine manual first published in New South Wales in 1830.

novel concrete foundations. His only remaining ambition, it said, was that his sons should grow up to be winemakers.

This last wish was not to be realized. The vineyard north of Wanganui failed to produce satisfactory wine grapes and a 200-acre (81-hectare) property purchased to the east of the town proved no better. In 1900 the Department of Agriculture warned settlers throughout the west coast that all the area from New Plymouth to Wellington was unsuited to viticulture. Soler's nephew, A.J. Vidal, who had gone to Palmerston North in 1900, and had unsuccessfully experimented with grapes at Hokowhitu, moved on to Hawkes Bay and for a time Soler's sons carried on the family business by buying grapes from the north. On the death of their father in 1906 they decided to go sheep farming.

The final triumph, however, was with Soler's Wanganui wine. The year the old Spaniard died there was a sensation at the Christchurch International Exhibition when his wines received three of the five gold medals in competition with overseas exhibitors. Leading Australian winemakers protested at this result and a special meeting of cabinet ordered a re-judging by an expert approved by the Australians. This time Soler's wines took all five gold medals.

Heinrich Breidecker of Hokianga

In 1870, 288 German immigrants landed at Port Chalmers, the first large group of that nationality to arrive since two hopeful shiploads had gone to Nelson to grow vines in the forties. These settlers, too, had been given expectations of grapes ripening under southern skies. They took up land in Canterbury, lived meagrely felling the isolated patches of bush in that province, and for a time made their own sauerkraut and parsnip wine and grew a little tobacco. But all their best vinegrowing efforts went unrewarded.

The faith of land speculators in the miracles to be worked by German skill and industry still lingered. J.D. Ormond, East Coast landowner and minister in the Fox cabinet, declared in 1871 that a proposed settlement of Nuhaka bush country was 'especially suited for Germans as the vine grows well there' and later said of the Mahia block: 'There the vine would grow splendidly and Germans would probably be the most suitable settlers.'

Perhaps Sir George Grey, who had successfully introduced German settlers to South Africa and South Australia and had sponsored winemaking there, was responsible for this optimism. He certainly had similar plans for New Zealand. Early in the New Zealand Wars his scheme to settle a thousand German military settlers in Taranaki was blocked at the last moment by the German authorities who objected to the recruitment of mercenaries and said their obligation to do road work at below current rates of wages resembled coolie importations to the West Indies.

The honour of Rhine winemakers was upheld finally, not by organised settlement but by the efforts of one man, Heinrich Breidecker, who planted a vineyard at New Plymouth in the seventies and then moved north to Hokianga.[4]

In the Hokianga, where vine runners climbed untended on old mission sites and around the abandoned gardens of early settlers, it was reported to the Native Department in 1884 that a German family had begun producing wine at Kohukohu. They were supplementing the harvest of their own vineyard with a ton of grapes picked from half-wild vines by Mangamuka River Maori and sold at two pence a pound. (For all their isolation, the Maori had keenly tuned their price to what the Spaniard Soler was paying Whanganui River Maori 725 kilometres to the south.)

Given the right grapes, Heinrich Breidecker said, he would make wine equal to the best on the Rhine. With his son Johann he broke in harsh land at Kohukohu, grew two acres of vines close to the ground along a low trellis of manuka poles and produced 'a good unadulterated wine' (according to a later Agriculture Department report) which sold readily at ten shillings a gallon.

The Breidecker press, home-made from local timber, had a moveable top of squared puriri cross-pieces operated by a bottle-jack and hand-woven willow baskets were sunk into the lees to draw off clear wine for casking. Prizes won for hock at the Dunedin Exhibition made good his claims for the methods of the Rhine.

There was a bad moment in 1888 when it was found that Breidecker was occupying crown land without title. 'I am so far now on a point where on the right side stands the asylums and on

---

4. Two Germans successfully applied to the newly formed Pukekura Park Board in 1875 for the lease of four acres for planting a vineyard. If one was Breidecker, his shift north could be explained by the board's requirement that the grounds were to be opened to the public at all times except for one month when the grapes were ripe.

the left hunger', he wrote to R. Allan Wight, a prominent horti-culturist, when the government showed no disposition to meet him reasonably. 'As there are no signs that I can obtain the land I think it is no use to keep my skill in a market where there is no want for it.'

Wight gave publicity to the case in the *Farmer:*

Now here is a man who has been very useful in his district, not only by showing his neighbours what he can do, but who has made a point of teaching them. And now the poor man, who seems to be completely dependent upon his little home-stead, is to lose all the fruits of his skill and labour, and to be turned out in his old age from a piece of land which, but for his improvements, would be of very little value.

The secretary of the Okaihau Agricultural and Horticultural Society had said that Breidecker's vineyard, the largest and best in the Bay of Islands district, was producing excellent wine, Wight wrote.

It is most obvious that practical men of this class are just precisely the very people we want in our warmer districts, and it would pay the Government over and over again to import as many of them as they can, and to make it well worth their while to come and settle amongst us.

Agreement was eventually reached and ten years later old Breidecker, white whiskers falling to his chest, received the governor, Lord Ranfurly, on his northern tour. Standing among vines running to hills thick with blackened stumps and still carrying dead trees on the skyline, he told how in good years he had taken as much as £400 from his two-acre patch of Isabellas and most seasons expected to make 1200 gallons of wine.

Others followed his example, among them a settler named Lester who, with help from a French workman, terraced an extremely steep hill face rising from the Kohukohu foreshore to plant the ledges in vine and orchard. But in 1913 when the Hokianga Chamber of Commerce issued a brochure extolling the virtues of the region, it could speak only of great expectations once held for the grape industry and Breidecker's thirty-year-old vines, then tended by his son Johann, were the only successful ones that could be mentioned.

FOR SALE.

At Moturata.

2 three-year-old colts by Albion
2 two-year-old fillies by Albion

Paspalum Seed next February
Moturata Wine in November

Address: C. SCHRADER,
Kohukohu.

Motukaraka Wine,
16/-, 18/-, 20/-. per case.

Cash with order.

None Genuine without my signature on Label.

E. TAFFORD,
Motukaraka. Hokianga.

Early advertisements for wines from the Hokianga.

The East Coast Hobbyists

Working in isolation, without private capital or state support, Levet, Soler and Breidecker had proved the possibilities of commercial winemaking. Before the century ended a group of gentleman-vignerons were to repeat the demonstration on another level.

All rich Hawkes Bay landowners, their interest in viticulture was sparked by William Beetham, second son and heir to 56,000 Wairarapa acres (22,680 hectares), who spent several years in France and as a young man brought back (along with a French wife from Picardy) a desire to see his own grapes being trodden in his own winehouse. In 1883 he planted an eighth of an acre in vines at his town house in Masterton, ultimately gathered up to the equivalent of nine tons of grapes to the acre, had his gardener tread the vintage, and began winemaking.

Beetham experimented with Pinot Noir, Pinot Meunier, Hermitage, Black Hamburgh, Black Muscat, Golden Chasselas and the white Spanish grape Doradillo. Over 3000 cuttings, mostly Pinots and some Hermitage, were transplanted to a three-acre vineyard named Lansdowne in 1892 and when a *Farmer* reporter called at vintage time five years later a team of children, working for two shillings a day, had just picked thirteen and a half tons of grapes from which Beetham's labourers had trodden 1850 gallons of wine.

The reporter commented:

No objection can sensibly be taken to the method of crushing by the feet. These are cleanly washed in warm water, and one might as well object to bread that is kneaded by the hands as to grapes trodden out for wine making. The best wines are made in this way, for the seeds of the grapes are not crushed and their acrid oil pressed out into the must, to its detriment for wine making, under the soft feet and limited weights of the treaders, whereas in crushing machines, should the seeds be nipped and smashed between the rollers, the wine is impaired.

The novelty, if not the profitability, of Beetham's hobby attracted other East Coast landowners to grape growing. Three with more than dilettante interest who were making wine by the mid-nineties were J.N. Williams of Frimley Orchards, Hastings; Bernard Chambers,

Te Mata Station, Havelock North; and Henry Tiffen, Greenmeadows Station, Taradale.

Williams, Beetham's brother-in-law, planted an acre of Pinot grapes in 1893, later expanded to seven acres; Chambers planted his first cuttings in 1892 after visiting vineyards in California, France and Australia and had two acres in vines five years later; and Tiffen, originally a New Zealand Company surveyor who had illegally occupied thousands of acres of Hawkes Bay Maori land in the fifties, made of his hobby the largest vineyard in the country.

In 1890, at the age of seventy-one a well-known public figure and prominent Anglican, Tiffen visited Masterton, lunched at Beetham's, tasted his wine, and saying (as the host later told the story) 'this is enough for me', returned to Taradale to spend a small fortune on planting a vineyard and building a model winery.

Tiffen sent his manager, S.F. Anderson, to Australia to study the industry and soon there were thirteen kilometres of wire trellis supporting ten acres (four hectares) of vines. At each vintage a small army of fifty or more children, selected from a still greater number of applicants, was turned loose at 7 a.m. for a nine-hour day of picking. A mechanised press-house carried the grapes by elevator to a second floor and fed them through stemming machines and crushers into a mobile wine press mounted on rails which emptied into a row of 1162-gallon totara fermenting vats — the only direct handling being that of a boy who shovelled the grapes on the elevator to begin the process.

A reporter who saw loads of barrels filled with grapes enter the Greenmeadows press-house during the 1895 vintage was moved to quote Byron:

Reeling with grapes, red waggons fill the way,
In England 'twould be dust, dung or a dray.

'It is evident to anyone that no expense has been spared to have everything the best of its kind', the Australasian fruit-growers' conference of 1896 was told in a report giving details of 'the premier vineyard of New Zealand'. There were then twenty-five acres (ten hectares) under vines with six more in preparation for planting. Beetham, who was present at the conference, said Tiffen's sideline, including a small orchard, had cost £9000.

That year Tiffen died and the Greenmeadows vineyard was taken over by his daughter, Mrs A.M. Randall, who carried on winemaking, expanding the area to thirty-five acres (fourteen hectares) by 1905, and then, influenced by a manager who had turned prohibitionist, began uprooting the vines and planting an orchard.[5] In 1921 Assid Corban's young son Wadier travelled to Greenmeadows and bought the contents of the winery, sending a whole train-load of barrels, bottling machines, crushers and other equipment back to Henderson.

After producing 4000 gallons of claret and hock for some years the vineyard at Frimley Orchards was similarly ploughed under when a syndicate that had taken over failed to make it pay.

Only Bernard Chambers' Te Mata Vineyard continued in existence, although greatly reduced in later years from the 1909 figures when there were thirty-five acres (fourteen hectares) under vines and the Australian manager, J.O. Craike (who won gold medals for Te Mata at the Franco-British and Japanese-British exhibitions), put down 12,000 gallons of claret, hock and madeira.[6]

Before the days of its decline Tiffen and Beetham would have appreciated the sight of Chambers sipping after-dinner wine with his family, French doors open to the summer evening, while across the rolling lawns Caccioppoli, an Italian worker from the vineyard, requested to stand well back because of the power of his voice, sang opera.

---

5. The portion of Greenmeadows purchased by the Mission after Tiffen's death had not included the area under vines or any winery buildings, only a stable which the brothers used as their first cellar. This picturesque wooden building was demolished (to the dismay of local artists and the history-conscious) between the author's visits to the district in January and August 1964.

6. In 1964 two vineyards occupied Te Mata land. A.J. Vidal leased and then bought seven acres of vines in 1922 and a remnant of the original, after languishing at the hands of a Wellington wine and spirit merchant in financial difficulties, ultimately passed to T.M.V. Wines Ltd, established in 1949.

The World of Wine — Marti Friedlander

Antonio Zame, Capri Vineyards, Gisborne (Italian).

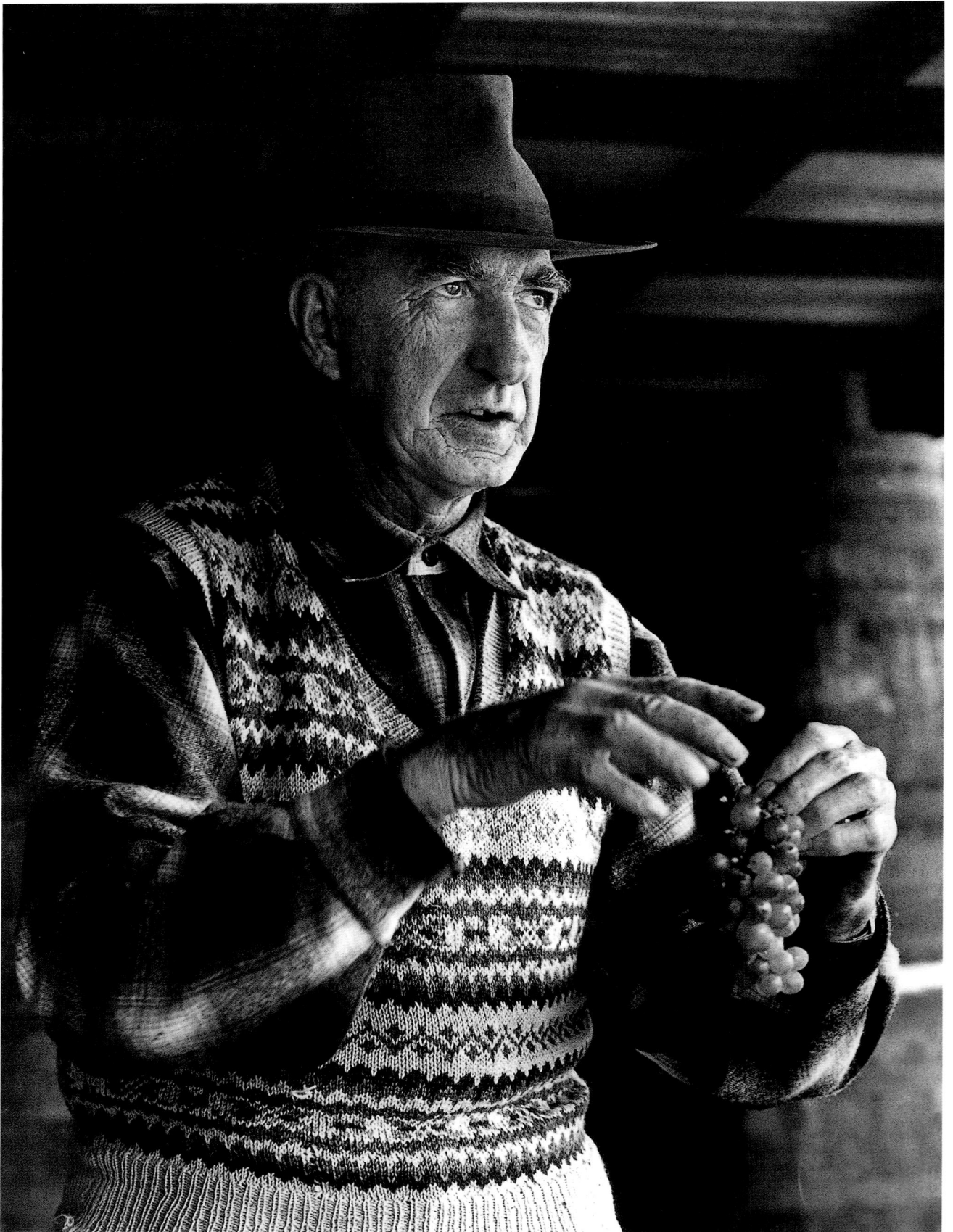

Frank Vidal, Vidal Wines, Hawkes Bay (Spanish).

Wadier and Khaleel Corban, Mt Lebanon Vineyards, Henderson (Lebanese).

Viggo Dufresne, Ruby Bay, Nelson (French/Danish).

Denis Kasza, always self-effacing (centre with dark glasses), McWilliams Wines, Hawkes Bay (Hungarian).

Victor Vladimir Zaremba, Muaga Vineyards, Henderson (Russian).

Friedrich Wohnsiedler, Waihirere Wines, Gisborne (German).

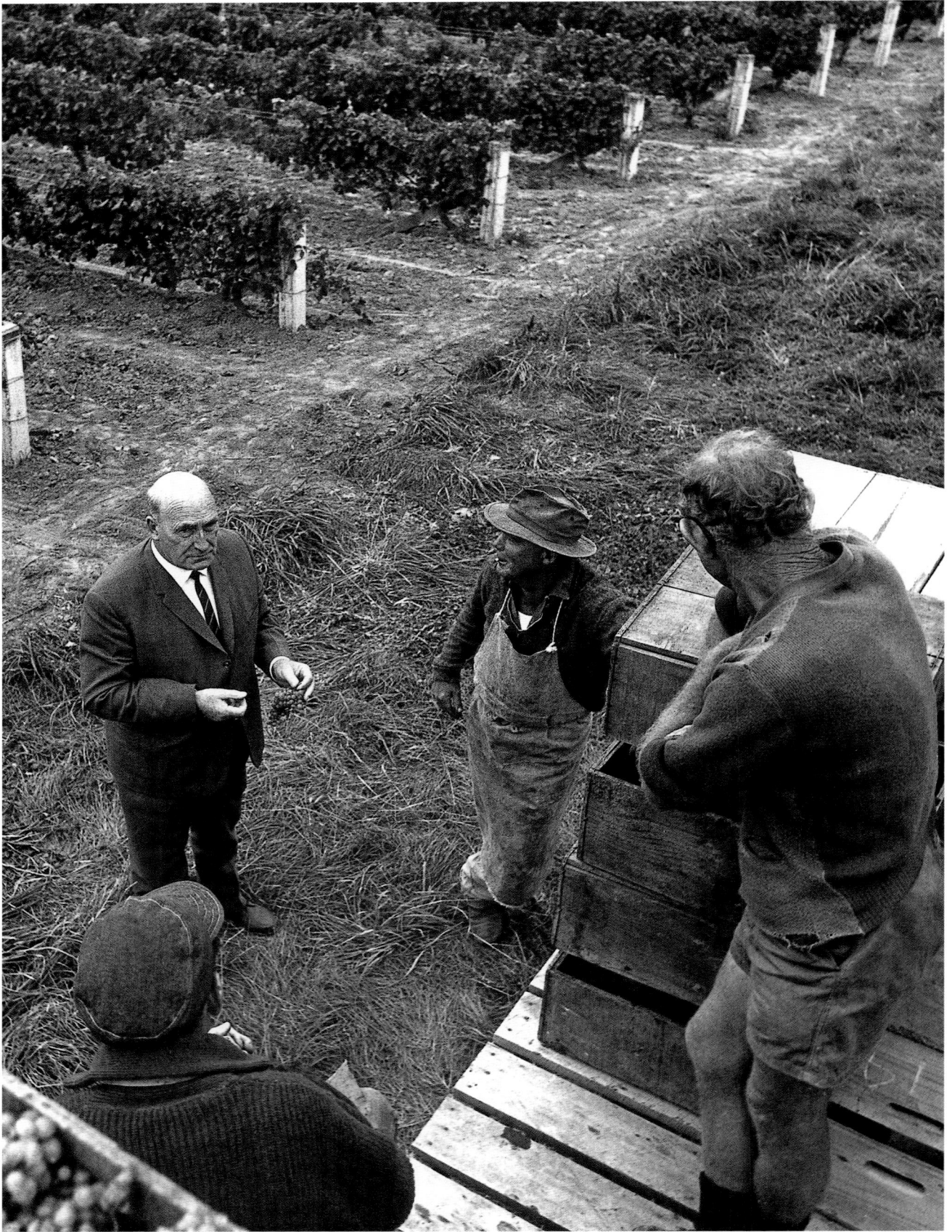

Tom McDonald, McWilliams Wines (Scottish).

Peter Hubscher, McWilliams Wines (Czech).

Joseph Babich, Babich's Vineyard, Henderson (Dalmatian).

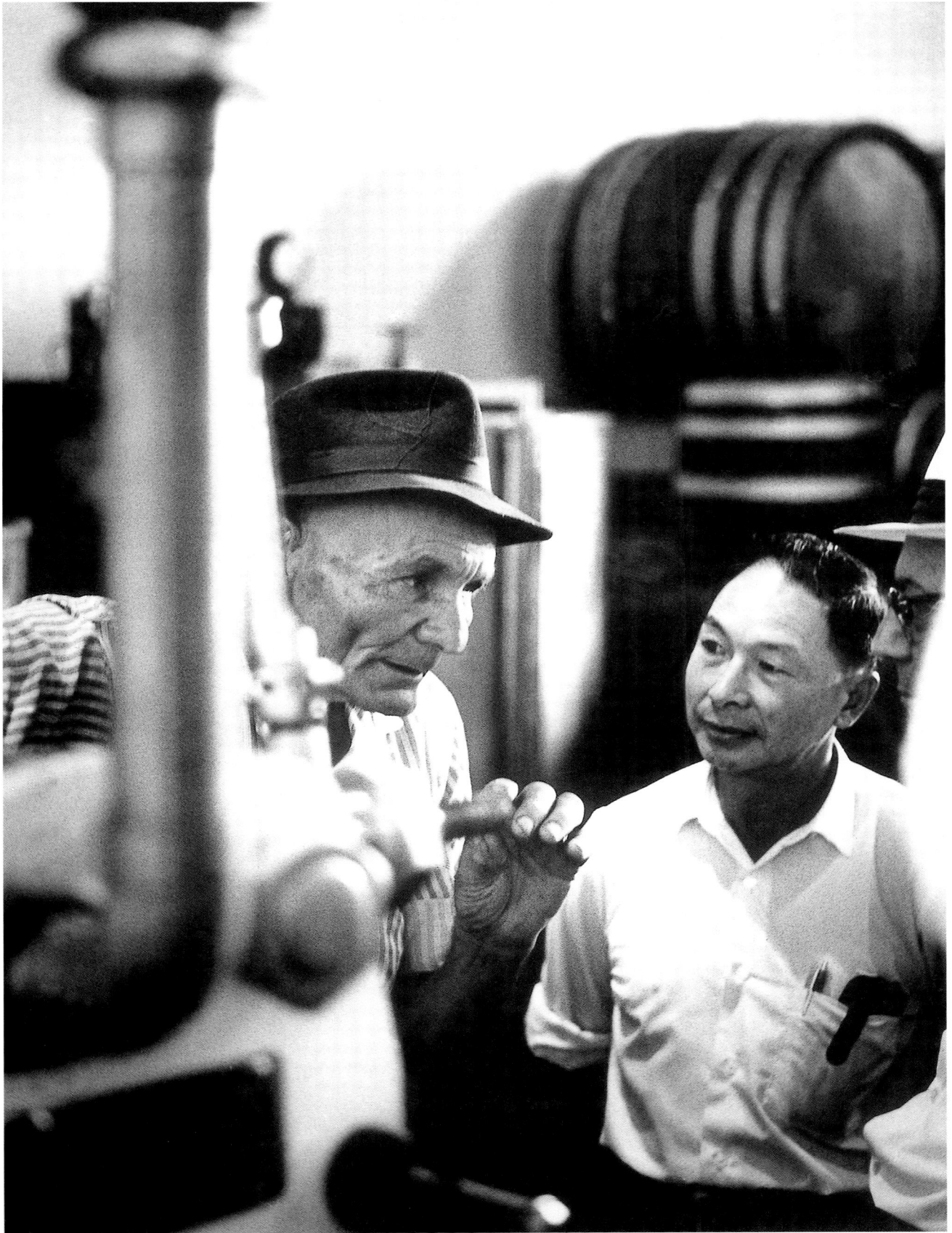

Joseph Babich and Stanley Chan, Totara Vineyards (Chinese).

Ulysse Lagiere, West Auckland vineyard worker (French).

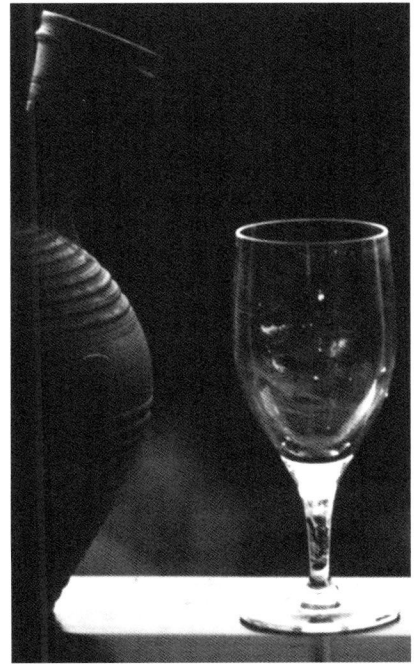

Orange Wine
and Rhubarb

For a poor man only grinding labour would To the North!

make a vineyard — a Spaniard, an Englishman

and a German had demonstrated that — and

the joyous wine festivals that beckoned the

first settlers to the South Seas had dissolved,

like Brodie's island of rock salt, at the first

touch of reality. Even the rich men of Hawkes

Bay had to depend on child labour or pay for

their songs. Yet in the last quarter of the century a new generation of pioneers was as ready for visions of plenty as their fathers. Short cuts to prosperity were what was wanted; for this there was a willingness to try anything and the air was thick with the schemes of charlatans, crack-brains, quick-profit merchants — even simple idealists — and the government, it seemed, was ready to lend an ear to them all.

Someone calculated what his wool cheque would be if Australian saltbush would thrive on the central North Island pumice deserts and the government cheerfully propagated 100,000 plants; someone else noticed the fashionably high price of ostrich feathers and the government fostered bird farms; a Bay of Islands farmer grazed his sheep on gorse and an Agriculture Department report declared 'prejudice is gradually being overcome' and (as late as 1899) recommended sowing, cultivating and manuring gorse plants in the same way as turnips. Rubber, tung oil, castor oil, opium, lavender — no product seemed too outlandish to entertain — and the cost of colonial innovation was high.

Typically, the Department of Agriculture planted at Te Kauwhata hundreds of acres in wattle to produce bark for tanning, discovered that thousands of trees were of the wrong variety that yielded no tannin, imported angora goats to stop them spreading and found the goats would eat almost anything — anything, that is, except the rampant seedlings.

In all this bumbling eagerness to find new products winemaking got less than its due. While Victoria subsidized its winegrowers £2 an acre to encourage new planting and South Australia met half the cost of new wineries, both plant and building, New Zealand's politicians were content to support extravagant schemes verbally and then leave the willing experimenter to battle unaided.

Sir George Grey, who as governor of South Australia had sent the first case of wine produced in that state to Queen Victoria in 1841, at least tried to match words with deeds in lending his influence to establishing a New Zealand wine industry. The Far North, roadless, virtually untried and seemingly tropical behind the mangroves, especially fired his imagination. As prime minister in 1879 he was responsible for having a large tract of land set aside for vineyards. The *Herald* reported:

The Waste Lands Board, at the instance of the government,

have reserved from sale a block of 26,000 acres in the Hokianga District, it being the object of Sir George Grey to establish there a settlement of skilled wine-growers, in order to regularly test the capacity of the colony for wine-production . . . The locality for the experiment has been well chosen, the climate of the northern districts of New Zealand being of course the most favourable.

Early in 1880 a Glasgow company promoter, George Galbraith, interviewed the New Zealand Agent-General in London, Sir Julius Vogel, with a proposal to settle vinegrowers from the south of France to organize a winemaking community if the government would provide free passage for his French settlers, build roads and railways and make the land available to his company at a cheap price on deferred payment. Winegrowing on small farms would support three to eight times the ordinary population, Galbraith argued — and this on land not otherwise usable. In his written offer, forwarded to New Zealand by Vogel, he quoted a French opinion to support his case:

> Bread and meat are consequences, and not causes of colon-ization; they constitute its necessities, and not its wealth; these being to population what wages are to workers — an expense, and not the treasury which provides the pay. The vine, on the contrary, is at once the workshop and the banker of the vignerons; it necessitates and forces all around the production of bread and meat, it pays a large tribute to the state, it exports afar its product, and finds still means largely to remunerate its proprietor if he is a true cultivator.

Although the chairman of the Hokianga County Council petitioned for special settlers following Grey's action, and although Galbraith's financial proposition was closely similar to that accepted from Colonel Feilding for his 'Manchester settlement' in the Manawatu, or from Vesey Stewart for his 'little Ulster' in the Bay of Plenty, no mass migration of Gallic winemakers enlivened the New Zealand scene.

Perhaps the government had seen enough of Frenchmen. In 1880, when the little schooner *Griffin* sailed up the Manukau from New Caledonia with a party of twenty Frenchmen on board, it had been greeted with the consternation due a hostile naval squadron, for the men who stepped ashore at Onehunga were ex-prisoners from the French penal colony — eleven of them Communards who had battled in the streets of Paris to defend the Commune of 1871. No law could be found to forbid the landing (even after nine years of confinement the politicals earned no more desperate adjectives than 'gentlemanly' or 'respectable' or 'smart and good-looking') and the wires burned with news of their movements. They were 'scattering in all directions in search of work', a police report stated, and as the hubbub died a press paragraph noted that Mr Dargaville, a bank manager turned merchant, had taken some of them north to grow vines for winemaking. None appeared on police files as a winemaker — their occupations ranged from professor of music to ship's carpenter — and it is possible that Dargaville, although of French Huguenot descent, shared the common English belief that all Frenchmen knew a great deal about viticulture.

Instead of promoting the introduction of foreigners, skilled or unskilled, the government embarked on a campaign to turn the north into a tropical garden — on the cheap. In 1882 James Pope, inspector-general of native schools, began distributing date palms, carob beans, olives, arrowroot plants, wattle seeds, mulberries and cinchona trees (source of quinine) for the teachers and their luckless pupils to cultivate.

In 1883 the government issued the substantial booklet *Silkworm Rearing* by an enterprising Italian, G.A. Federli, demonstrating that groves of mulberries would support silkworms and so a silk industry. His instructions were complete with fold-out plans of a silk-spinning machine but the *New Zealand Farmer* of the day thought his advice 'not a reliable guide for colonists to follow'.

In 1884 the *Treatise and Handbook of Orange Culture* by Whangarei orchardist and vinegrower George Alderton was published by the government printer. It carried on its title page this verse:

North Auckland:
Know'st thou the land where the lemon-trees bloom,
Where the gold orange glows in the deep thicket's gloom,
Where a wind ever soft from the blue heavens blows,
And the groves are of miro and nikau and rose?

A hardcover book, the 'treatise' proclaimed that oranges could be grown at high, if vaguely stated, profit and also made into wine:

Given a suitable site and other circumstances favourable, the crop will pay four times better than anything else you can grow. It is no use going into figures; they at best would be purely imaginary, as different circumstances would govern every case. No doubt fortunes are to be made, and have been made, from orange-growing, but that does not necessarily imply that all orange-cultivation must pay. As a matter of fact, very many persons have tried to grow oranges and failed most egregiously.

Slightly more specific were details about the wine taken from a Californian source:

Orange wine is of an amber colour, tastes like dry hock, but retains for ever the aroma of the orange. From the cakes which I took out of the press, I made vinegar, with an addition of water and molasses . . . and, from the peels, oil of orange or an extract of orange could be made, and so every particle of that delicious fruit can be utilized.

Orange tree at Whangarei producing 200 dozen fruit a year — the frontispiece to Alderton's *Treatise and Handbook of Orange Culture*. The man up the ladder is from the *Colonist's Guide*.

ORANGE WINE
AND RHUBARB

The economics were clear enough: 'A good workman can peel and squeeze a hundred and twenty oranges in one hour . . . One thousand two hundred sour oranges and one thousand five hundred bitter-sweet or sweet oranges make one barrel of forty-five gallons of wine, and ten gallons of vinegar.' More attractive than peeling onions, it could have been said, but Alderton's orange-wine industry was as still-born as the others.

In 1885–86 Pope, Federli and Alderton were continuing the good work. Pope reported that 'the work of introducing useful plants into Native districts is being steadily carried forward'. Federli, who had planned an Italian settlement of vignerons as well as silk farmers at Hokianga, arrived with his wife and two Englishmen to take up land near Rangiahua. Twenty more settlers were to follow from Christchurch. 'I am afraid Federli is a visionary, and will not do much,' the local magistrate, von Sturmer, wrote to a friend in 1885: 'Had he got his original scheme off, of the Italians, he might have succeeded.' Von Sturmer was right. Next year he reported that the Italian had abandoned the land and was 'maturing his plan re sanatorium at Opononi; he is a very wily customer, and if any person could succeed he is the man. I have put my small piece in his hand.' A week later Federli had left for Wellington, a writ for a £100 debt behind him.[1]

That same year Alderton received a government grant of two months' travelling expenses to investigate the wine industry of the United States. His lengthy report published by the government was of the calibre of his orange 'treatise' and consisted almost entirely of reprinted American material. A year was wanted to do the job properly, he said, but this did not deter him from firm conclusions: 'I see no reason why people here should not amass the same large fortunes as have been made in California.' In fact, New Zealand winegrowers had the advantage:

> The quality of our climate is not appreciated, and, while crowds of English people are going to California and Florida to engage in fruit-culture, our colony is never thought of for

---

1. It was reported by a *Farmer* correspondent in 1902 that of the people induced by 'an Italian gentleman' to join a settlement at Hokianga 'there are at present about half a dozen of these settlers still there, two of them, I understand, have planted small vineyards, but most of them go in for ordinary fruit growing'.

such a purpose. But were its merits more fully known in England — that we have here a climate surpassed by none in the world, and a country free from every kind of reptile — how many would then go to Florida with its malarial climate, its rivers swarming with crocodiles, and its jungles with the most deadly snakes; or to Southern California, the home of the dreaded tarantula!

Meanwhile, outside the rhetoric, wine was being made in Northland. In addition to a sprinkling of Frenchmen who had taken up viticulture, the German, Heinrich Breidecker, was already selling wine at Hokianga. What these practical men wanted from the government was not flights of prose on spiders, snakes and crocodiles but a few legal phrases giving them the right to distil their own wine spirits . . .

A machine for washing oranges recommended by the Department of Agriculture in 1898.

The Distilling Debate

The first attempt to amend the law to allow the distillation of wine spirits was made by Sir George Grey in 1888. He failed to get the bill considered by parliament that year but Joseph Soler of Wanganui kept the issue alive and the German and French winemakers of the north waited on their local member (Marsden electorate) to support his representations.

Soler presented a strong case to a parliamentary committee set up to investigate the industry in 1890, arguing that winemakers could not afford to use imported spirits to fortify their product when the duty was £1.4.0 a gallon. Nor could they afford, he said, to wait seven years as he was doing before selling their wine in order that it could build up its own alcoholic strength. In fact, wine decreases in alcoholic content with time but it was a plausible argument. Chaired by George Beetham, member for Masterton and brother of Wairarapa winemaker William Beetham, the committee found that the industry was capable of extensive development, even on otherwise unproductive land, and to assist this growth recommended that the Distilling Act be amended as requested.

A bill was introduced the same year to allow vineyards of two acres or more to install stills of twenty-five to fifty gallons for fortifying wine up to an alcohol content of forty per cent. The

provisions exactly followed Australian legislation, a government speaker explained, and spelt out the need for the measure in these words:

> No matter in what country, there were certain seasons when grapes and fruit would not produce wine of sufficient strength to keep it in good condition, to mature it and enable it to ripen and become an article fit for export or consumption. The cause of this was sometimes increased moisture, want of sun and warmth, or cold nights; and the grapes would not contain sugar in sufficient quantities, and, no matter whether in France, Spain, Victoria, Adelaide, or anywhere else, this wine would have to be fortified and strengthened by spirits distilled from the products of the grape and in that way matured and given the strength, body and flavour required.

As the industry was to learn by bitter experience in the years ahead a smooth passage for the most reasonable reform was more than could be expected from parliament. One member wanted to establish a big distillery for making all kinds of spirits and so not 'allow mere play, as it were, with a few grapes'. Another, who spoke as a total abstainer and had at first overlooked the item on the order paper 'owing to the strong light and late hours they kept', rallied to oppose it from another flank. Only one or two wanted the legislation, he said, and in obvious reference to Joseph Soler went on to elaborate; 'Take the case of a gentleman who grew grapes, say, two hundred miles up-country . . . it would be necessary that some Customhouse Officer should go all the way up-country now and then to make an inspection.' Then in self-contradiction he visualized many taking advantage of the legislation; 'Let this instance be multiplied . . . and . . . that would entail a very large amount of extra expense upon the colony.'

John Ballance, member for Wanganui, answered the suggestion that Soler alone would benefit. Not only his own district but also North Auckland stood to gain, he said. But the Bay of Islands representative, Richard Hobbs, no inheritor of local Busby tradition, said it was 'a perfect farce' to talk about winemaking in New Zealand. It would be far better to bring in Australian wines 'than to manufacture a lot of rubbish in this country'. The debate, never remarkable for its logic, broke down at this point into personality exchanges about the honourable members' drinking habits — a diversion which ended with Hobbs solemnly placing on record in *Hansard* that he had given up whisky drinking seven years previously, a moving testimony which another member attempted to mar by saying that he had seen the speaker in Bellamys 'carrying a very suspicious parcel, something like a bottle of whisky rolled up', only the previous week.

Parliament voted on this note, the 'wets' winning by thirty-seven to nineteen. In the upper house the 'drys' were ready for sterner battle. Robert Pharazyn dismissed the proposal as 'a mere pretext for the establishment of illicit stills'; Dr Grace said there was 'really no manufacture of wine worth talking about in the colony' and any that was attempted 'would be eked out with the use of rhubarb'. Rhubarb also worried the next speaker, W.H. Reynolds, who said that 'if they allowed the bill to pass anyone could get up two acres of supposed vineyard — it might be a rhubarb garden . . . there might not be more than one hundred vines and the rest might be filled up with rhubarb or gooseberries . . . '

In some disgust the only speaker in support of the measure said it could not be supposed that there would be such imbecility on the part of the supervising customs authorities as to not notice this subterfuge but by ten votes to five the bill was rejected. The following year John Ballance became prime minister. When he personally re-introduced an identical bill it quickly passed the lower house again and this time the upper house found it discreet not to stand in the way.

Exhausted by the distilling battle, its first worthwhile effort to aid winemaking, the government pushed the industry's problems aside until a proposed free-trade treaty with South Australia in 1895 brought winegrowers into prominence again. A number of growers gave evidence against the importation of duty-free Australian wines. They protested that free trade would ruin them although some bold spirits said they would have nothing to fear from Australian competition if only the law were amended to allow them to sell by the bottle.

In the South Island at this time Freeth and Company of Mt Pleasant, near Picton, were making 1000 gallons of wine a year, a quarter of it grape-wine selling in bulk at 6/6 to 7/6 a gallon, and the rest currant, gooseberry, elderberry, blackberry and apple wines selling at one shilling a gallon less; F.H.M. Ellis and Sons at

Motupipi, near Takaka, were substantial winemakers; E.C. Mouldey made red wine from four acres of grapes at Christchurch and had 8000 gallons in store; Joseph Mandl, mayor of Hokitika, one of three fruit-wine manufacturers in that town, had been in business twenty years and made thirty to forty quarter casks annually; Christopher and Peter Frank, winemakers in Nelson since the early seventies, had one acre of Golden Chasselas.

North Island winemakers not previously mentioned included P. LeQuesne of Hamilton, a Jersey Islander who had been buying grapes from Waikato settlers and making wine for seven years — on one occasion breaking through the tight barrier of wine and spirit merchants by selling 500 gallons to Campbell and Ehrenfried; a newly formed wine manufacturing company at Takapuna was selling through the Albert Hotel, Auckland; L.L. Kingdon, Omata, Taranaki, was making 'an excellent port'; at isolated Helena Bay, halfway between Whangarei and the Bay of Islands, a group of Swiss settlers had been making wine since the eighties, selling 'a capital claret' at six shillings a gallon.

The tariff commission reported that from Auckland to Otago there were winemakers with stocks of from 4000 to 8000 gallons of New Zealand wine 'of a very palatable nature' but nevertheless recommended that free trade would bring greater advantages than support of a local wine industry. Before the death sentence could be put into effect, however, the South Australian parliament failed to ratify the treaty and winemakers celebrated their reprieve by basking in the praises of an Italian expert brought in to report on their industry.

Wine and water in enamel mugs for Dalmatian diggers during a work break on a northern gumfield — except for one boy too exhausted to take his share. This group is typical of the men who turned in earnest to winemaking when their spears eventually failed to bottom on paying quantities of kauri gum.

Simon Ujdur, early Viticultural Association president, whose West Auckland Birdwood Vineyard founded in 1915 once ranked with Corbans and Vidals as one of the country's big three.

The last of the gumdigger-winemakers, Tony Yelash, holds to the past on a lonely plateau behind Ahipara in the Far North. He insisted on wearing a suit to pose for Bernie Hill's photographs published in *Wine Review*, 1966.

Tony Yelash's corrugated iron shack and patch of
vines, the only mark of man in thousands of
acres of abandoned gumland.

A bleak winter's day does not deter Ivan Markovina (literally 'Mark of the Wine') from pruning and tying his precious vines. Family records begin with seventeenth-century winemaking on the island of Korcula off the Dalmatian coast and show a gold medal won at a Paris exhibition in 1912. The founder of Markovina Vineyards, Kumeu, came to New Zealand as a boy of sixteen.

(SIMON BUIS, *WINE REVIEW*)

Peter Fredatovich, founder of Lincoln Vineyards, fascinates school children with a rich harvest from vines first trained on an overhead trellis a quarter of a century before. Beside the barrels he had once shaped and steamed with handmade tools he could point out his stainless-steel still, the first installed by a New Zealand winemaker.

Jova Rancich, gumdigger turned Titirangi potter, made the richly glazed wine jar inscribed with winemaker Simon Ujdur' s name, one of many he produced for the vineyard.

(MARTI FRIEDLANDER PHOTOGRAPHS)

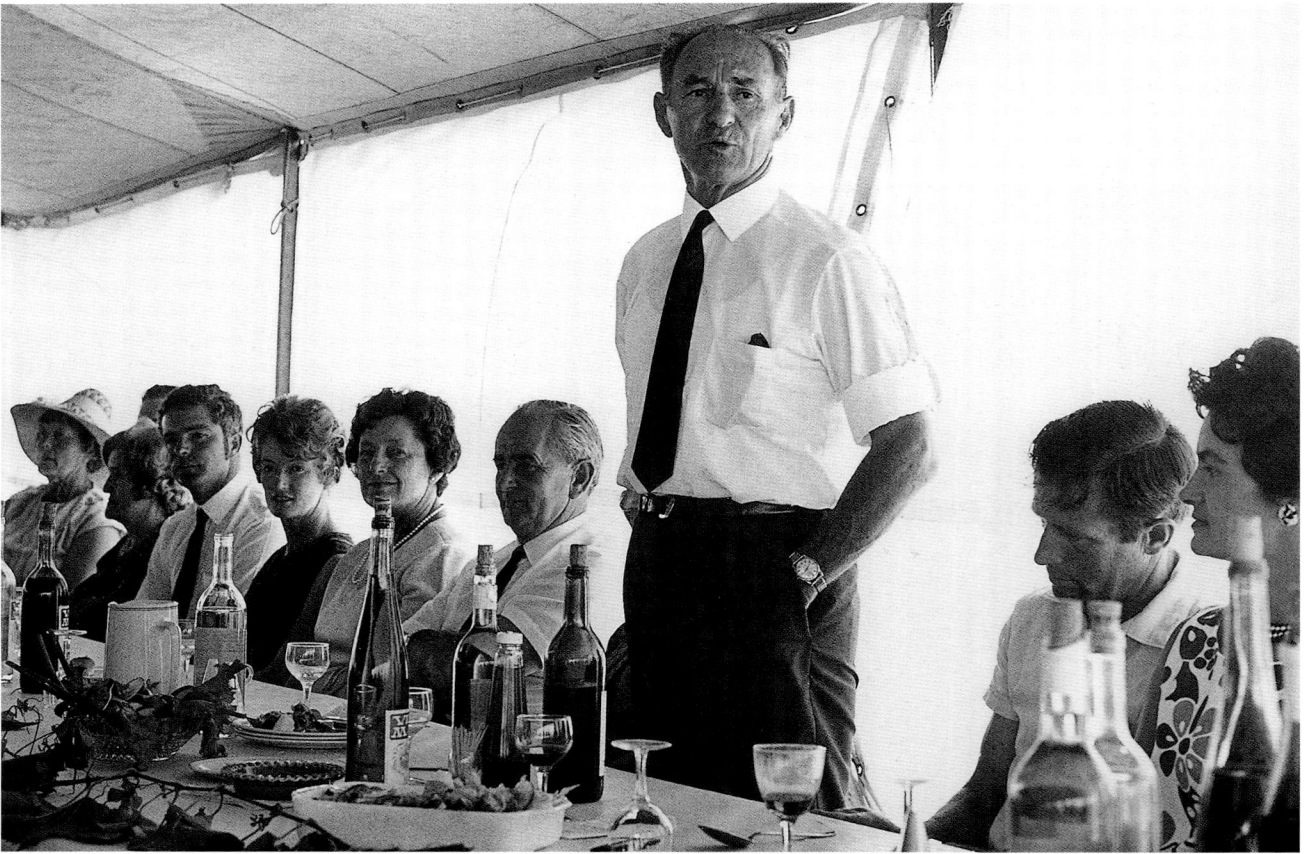

George Mazuran, the winemakers' tireless political lobbyist, presides at the Viticultural Association's 1970 field day. George Fistonich, Villa Maria Vineyards, is seated fourth from left.

(Marti Friedlander)

Planning golden jubilee celebrations, the association's executive meets in 1966. From left: Nick Delegat, Victor Talijanich, Martin White, Peter Fredatovich (secretary), George Mazuran (president), Mate Brajkovich (vice-president), Peter Babich (vice-president), Michael Jelas, Nick Nobilo, Mate Selak.

Folk music from Dalmatia for the 1968 field day, while barbecued lamb and local wines vanish from tables in the big top at Vitasovich's Ideal Vineyard, Henderson. Diana Mazuran played the accordion and Tony Marinovich sang and played guitar. 'Is it a love song?' the author asked a winemaker's wife. 'Yes,' she said, 'it always makes me cry.'

(MARTI FRIEDLANDER)

Nick Delegat carves, Nick Nobilo (left) waits a turn and John Rae, MP, looks on.

OPPOSITE

Three of the full muster from parliament for the 1968 field day: from left, Dr Martyn Findlay, MP, Matiu Rata, MP, and Alan Highet, MP, with wine merchant Graeme Reid and winemaker Mate Selak at right.

OPPOSITE BELOW

An experienced hand with the knife: Minister of Finance Robert Muldoon takes over the carving, flanked by Whetu Tirikatene-Sullivan, MP, and Hugh Watt, deputy leader of the opposition.

(MARTI FRIEDLANDER PHOTOGRAPHS)

Nick Delegat and Mate Selak take readings from a co-operatively owned experimental brandy still while a customs officer, Warren Leonard, stands by.

(MARTI FRIEDLANDER)

OPPOSITE

Frank Yukich receives Montana's first gold medal from Industries and Commerce officer Ken Davies.

OVERLEAF

A gold medal for George and Florence Mazuran's dessert wine.

The Overseas Expert

Romeo Bragato Reports

Which was the best wine district? One southern champion told the Canterbury Industrial Association in 1887 'the future wine country *par excellence* will be the interior of Otago . . . the appearance even of the country favours the idea; the slopes of the ranges in the Dunstan district always remind me of the views I have seen of the wine districts in Spain and Portugal.' Another regional partisan saw in

'The majority of the people of New Zealand do not appear to have any conception of the enormous wealth-producing capabilities of Central Otago. It is, however, hardly to be expected that people will of free choice invest money, expend labour and live a comparatively isolated existence when the field of choice is so wide as it is today.' Romeo Bragato reporting to Richard John Seddon on the prospects of viticulture in New Zealand, 1895.

Hawkes Bay hills 'the peculiar truncated appearance of the vine-clothed hills of the celebrated Côte d'Or district in France' and declared that here was 'the most suitable wine-producing district'. Joseph Soler told a parliamentary committee there was no better place than the upper Whanganui River, Picton winemaker Freeth swore by the Marlborough Sounds and, as we have seen, no area had more pressing advocates than North Auckland. What would Romeo Bragato say?

In 1895 Bragato, an Italian viticulturist employed by the government of Victoria, was loaned to New Zealand to report on the suitability of the different districts. His tour began at Bluff in February and he tasted his first glass of New Zealand wine at Arrowtown, Central Otago, a few days later. 'Although made after the most primitive fashion,' he later reported to the prime minister, Seddon, 'it reflected great credit upon the producer, and need not be despised by any one.' At Cromwell and Clyde he saw many vines growing outdoors and found grapes already fully ripe by 25 February, 'a convincing fact to me that the summer climatic conditions here are conducive to the early ripening of the fruit'. Small orchards and vineyards had been established in this region by goldminers working the Clutha who abandoned their claims each summer when the river rose, and Bragato was full of admiration for these 'singularly lion-hearted' men who had to take their fruit and table grapes from forty to seventy miles (up to 112 kilometres) by dray to the nearest rail-head.[1] Central Otago was 'pre-eminently suitable,' he decided, 'and there does not appear to me any statable limit to the productiveness of that magnificent territory.'

At Akaroa and again at Nelson Bragato gave similar verdicts. He noted that Lower and Upper Moutere were the best placed for growing oak trees that he had seen since leaving Europe and with rising enthusiasm made this recommendation:

The Government would, in my opinion, be taking a decidedly wise step were it to determine in the near future to convert portions of these districts into oak forests, in view of the possibility of New Zealand becoming a large wine-producing

---

1. As early as 1881 Vincent Pyke, goldfields member, told the House that J.D. Feraud of Monte Cristo, near Clyde, was sending wines, bitters and liqueurs to Dunedin and had won awards at Sydney and Melbourne exhibitions.

colony. It will be readily conceded that it would be a great national advantage to be able to draw upon your own forest for the oak timber required for making staves for casks and other wine-making utensils.

After hospitality in Wellington, Bragato was accompanied by three Agriculture Department officials to Beetham's Wairarapa vineyard. He inspected three acres of wine grapes, found them in perfect condition and drank some prime-quality six-year-old Hermitage wine. At Greenmeadows, the twenty-two-acre Tiffen vineyard had produced a magnificent crop of Pinot, the finest grapes Bragato had seen. A visit to four other vineyards in the same area and he decided that Hawkes Bay and Wairarapa were also great wine-country. 'I look forward to the time when these provinces will be studded with vineyards,' he reported to Seddon.

The Bay of Plenty, Whangarei, Waikato and Wanganui then received the expert's approval. Winegrowing taken up with spirit at all these places, he declared, assured a handsome reward to the grower and the country at large.

The final verdict was entirely favourable: 'The land in your colony, if properly worked, should yield a very large quantity of grapes per acre from which wine of the finest quality, both red and white and champagne could be produced.' It required only that growers form associations to select the best grape varieties and to control planting and the marketing of the product, and 'each district would subsequently gain notoriety for the wine produced, as in the various famed wine districts of the Continent'.

There was an immediate response to Bragato's optimism. His suggestion of co-operative effort, in particular, was in tune with ideas already successfully applied in the dairy industry. At a conference of Australian and New Zealand fruitgrowers in Parliament Buildings, Wellington, in 1896 (at which three of the four papers on viticulture were delivered by enthusiastic New Zealanders) a prominent Whangarei vinegrower, Lionel Hanlon, echoed Bragato's advice:

The absurdity of every man who has an acre or two of vineyard manufacturing so-called port, sherry, bordeaux, burgundy, chablis, tokay, etc., need not be discussed. It cannot too forcibly be impressed upon the future winegrowers of

New Zealand the great importance of each district producing a class of wine of definite type. Viticultural associations could be formed in each district and the growers should then agree amongst themselves to produce not more than one red and one white class of wine; and let them boldly from the first be named from the district in which they are grown, and not ape the names of celebrated vintages of Europe.

A Central Otago Vine and Fruitgrowers' Association had already been formed when Bragato stopped at Dunedin to address a public meeting on his way back to Australia. (The vineyards could be irrigated by converting the miners' sluicing gear, he said, and winemaking would return £100 an acre in five years.) Now a North Auckland Vinegrowers' Association was organised. With better prospects of success — the 'Vine' was later dropped from the Otago title — this association distributed 30,000 imported vine cuttings to its fifty members in 1897 in order to establish the varieties best suited to each district. The president, R.E. Fenton, alone experimentally planted over 4000 cuttings of thirty different European varieties on his newly established eight-acre Kaipara vineyard.

A son of Judge F.D. Fenton of the Native Land Court who had retired to the Kaipara in the eighties to grow wine grapes, Fenton shared his father's belief in the industry's great future. He could see co-operation going even further than Bragato had envisaged. Interviewed by an Auckland daily he said:

> The North Auckland Vinegrowers' Association has really made its object the maintaining of a co-operative spirit among the growers. It is estimated in Australia that it will not pay a man with less than 20 acres under vines to go in for making his own wine, and most of the Northern growers will not put down anything like such an area as that. One of the objects of the association is, therefore, to establish a factory on the co-operative principle, when the adaptability of the grape is more fully tested and so obviate small growers having to make their own wine.

Bragato had painted in bold strokes, the growers were brushing in the detail; in a perfect picture there was only one flaw — phylloxera.

In Auckland, at two Mt Eden vineries, Bragato had found over a hundred vines infected with the aphids that had almost wiped out the wine industry of France. Phylloxera aphids had established themselves in French vineyards during the Franco-Prussian war of 1870 and had caused more economic damage than the war itself. In less than ten years three and three quarter million acres of vines had been destroyed out of a total of five million and all of Europe was threatened until it was discovered that vines grown on American roots would resist attack. For New Zealand, phylloxera was still something of the mystery it had been when Frenchmen first saw the vines turn pale and die and wondered if it was God's punishment for having deserted the emperor. Its complex life cycle had been uncovered by European scientists, insecticide treatment had been tried and abandoned, by 1890 France had replanted over half its vineyards with resistant grafted vines — but New Zealand still clung to old remedies.

The presence of phylloxera had first been suspected in 1885 when sickly vines in a Remuera glasshouse were destroyed after having gone untreated for four years. Professor Thomas Kirk, a university botanist called in by the government, was sceptical of the identification and complacently reported that 'so long as the importation of vines is prohibited, there is but little danger of the vine-louse reaching the shores of the colony. Even should an importation take place the insect may be prevented from spreading by prompt adoption of destructive measures.'

When the aphids again appeared in 1889–90 at Auckland and Whangarei a bill was drafted for the compulsory destruction of diseased vines but parliament could see no emergency and a well-known horticulturist, R. Allan Wight, was appointed to persuade owners voluntarily to burn infected vines and quick-lime the soil. Not all would agree to such drastic action and Wight found growers 'much against legislation and indeed the objection to interference with the management of one's orchard or one's vines is universal'. He was even powerless to act against a nurseryman who had distributed infested vines.[2]

---

2. Wight reported to the Minister of Agriculture that phylloxera-infested vines had been smuggled ashore in a carpet bag four years before and delivered to this Auckland nurseryman 'who boasted of the transaction'. A year later when judging the Whangarei Show, he had given out a dozen of these vines as prizes.

A typical settler's attitude to compulsion was expressed by G.E. Alderton of Whangarei who told the government after the first outbreak:

> Some people think this nuisance should be suppressed by act of parliament but this is impossible . . . To make a hard-and-fast law, giving any one power to destroy any shrub or tree or hedge upon which a pest had settled, if it were ˎnot eradicated, would be altogether too arbitrary and unpopular.

Alderton considered 'Boards of Horticultural Commissioners' should be appointed.

> These Boards, of course, would be composed of practical fruit-growers whose interest it would be to suppress the insect nuisance as a measure of mutual protection, and who, in doing so, would never dare to resort to too harsh measures lest they pickle a rod which subsequently would be applied to themselves.

By delaying drastic action hundreds of vinegrowers, not least Alderton, were pickling quite a rod for themselves.

Positive identification of phylloxera by Bragato in 1895 at last galvanised the government into action. A Phylloxera Act was passed giving wide powers for the destruction of infested vines. Half a dozen inspectors were appointed to search the country, in some districts house-to-house, for phylloxera. They combed gardens, glasshouses, vineyards and even uprooted vines growing wild up hillsides and in remote valleys. Given power to enter any land, premises, conveyances or vessels, the inspectors could seize, destroy or disinfect any vines. And any person committed an offence 'who directly or indirectly obstructs, hinders, or interrupts or threatens, or assaults or uses improper or abusive language to an inspector and his assistants'.

'I need hardly remind you that tact and reticence are desirable in order to avoid friction and prevent a scare,' the head of the horticulture division of the Department of Agriculture told his inspectors, but friction — and heat — were inevitable. An irate George Alderton protested to a parliamentary committee:

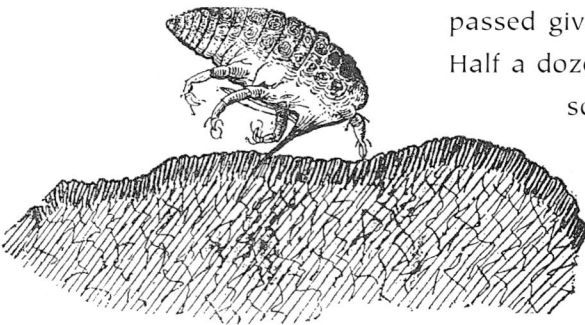

Phylloxera sucking tube in a vine root.

The greatest blight that has ever befallen on the fruit industry is not of the bug species. It is the interference of the government through an army of inspectors. These parasites are harder to get rid of than all the bugs. The law does not permit us to spray them with their only certain specific — buck-shot . . . Under the present law no one but a lunatic would think of planting a vineyard; it would simply mean placing one's self sooner or later in the clutches of the inspector.

Knapsack spraying of vines in 1891. The filled tank weighed 50 pounds, 'quite heavy enough for a man to carry about all day ...'

After Alderton's small vineyard was destroyed he never planted another and apart from an abortive attempt in 1902 to float a company for making 'Orange Quinine Wine' and 'Sparkling Grape Wine' the expert of the eighties was not heard of again.

Some winemakers suffered heavy losses. One Bay of Plenty vineyard of seven acres at Katikati was totally destroyed, together with several thousand rooted cuttings ready for transplanting. The owner, an experienced New South Wales viticulturist, had been just on the point of advertising the cuttings for sale throughout New Zealand when the aphids were discovered. 'He justly complained,' the vine inspector reported, 'that while he had paid high prices for vines of special varieties, few proved true to name, and he had been abundantly stocked with phylloxera and black spot.'

The phylloxera aphid was all but invisible, only one millimetre in length, but there was something personal about the campaign waged against it. The 'vine louse' and its parts, greatly enlarged, were demonstrated by lantern slides (sometimes provoking a respectful response from settlers not aware of the possibilities of magnification) and the language of description heightened the effect. A department report reads:

The most important organ of all, in its relation to the vine, and the weapon which causes all the mischief, is the rostrum or needle-shaped beak, which is thrust to one-third of its length into the young rootlet, on which the insect thus fastens itself, while the sap rises by capillary force into this hollow and pointed mouthpiece, which is so articulated that it can either remain flat against the body of the insect or stand erect, as when ready to pierce the tissues of the roots or of the leaf of the vine, as may be. The newly born phylloxera, under the compulsion of circumstances which have not yet been sufficiently threshed out, either crawl towards the upper surface of the young leaves, on which they can attach themselves by means of their beak to the leaf, forming a gall on the spot (hence the name 'gallicole' given to this form) or make for the roots, and for this reason are called 'radicole'.

At the winged stage, the report said: 'It is armed with powerful eyes, containing many lenses, which apparently enable it to detect vines at a long range of vision, as well as long antennae or feelers with auditive and smelling or tactile glands, which seem to be of use in its distribution.' At another metamorphosis a wingless form emerged without feeding organs or rostrum — 'the whole of their attention is thus concentrated towards love-making' — and at yet another 'the females deposit their solitary egg, an operation accompanied with violent contractions of the mother's body, who exhausted, dies alongside the egg she had brought forth'.

Captain T. Broun, a vine inspector who claimed the honour of finding the first winged phylloxera in New Zealand, told a grower's conference that he had been home for only five days in the first seven months of the eradication campaign and 'these five days were devoted to departmental work'. In volcanic soil at Mt Eden, in deep alluvium at Opotiki and in stiff clay at Whangarei he had found 'the dreaded phylloxera'.

By 1899 a hundred infested properties had been discovered, the majority growing only a few vines. Forty-three of these were within a few kilometres of Whangarei and most of the remainder were in Auckland Province. Six infested places were located in Wellington Province and even Hawkes Bay, regarded as a phylloxera-free district, did not escape.[3]

Eradication was an expensive, painstaking process. Here are the instructions given a Wairarapa inspector to destroy three small vineyards near Masterton:

---

3. The Agriculture Department reported in 1900: 'Phylloxera was found on a few very old vines in a thoroughly isolated position in Hawkes Bay. These were at once destroyed and the most careful search throughout the province did not result in the discovery of any others.'

(1) cut down the vines and burn them; (2) pour a little kerosene down the stumps, to kill any nymphs should they be working their way to the surface; (3) inject (in the soil) small doses of carbon bisulphide and kerosene at short distances, and at intervals of a few days; (4) after an interval of about a fortnight dig up and burn the roots; (5) inject further doses of carbon in order to make absolutely certain that no insect should escape.

The government bore the cost of destruction but met none of the growers' losses. This was compared unfavourably with compensation to dairy farmers of two-thirds the market value for diseased cattle compulsorily destroyed and on one critic's calculation, payment of at least £160 an acre should have been made when vines over three years old were uprooted. A member of parliament produced the case of a widow who had lost all her income of £250 a year when her vineyard was destroyed 'and received not a penny in compensation'. Bending to pressure the department avoided conflict by using carbon bisulphide in an effort to save condemned areas. One-ounce doses were repeatedly injected into the soil at yard intervals throughout infested vineyards — a costly treatment continued until 1901 although long discredited overseas.

Bragato had made two phylloxera recommendations in 1895: that all vines in the country be inspected in order to destroy infested plants and that American resistant vines be imported from Europe by the Department of Agriculture for distribution to growers. The department's Momohaki experimental farm at Waverley, thirty-two kilometres north of Wanganui, did begin free distribution of cuttings in 1896 — but not of resistant varieties — and the following year when the vines were first planted at Te Kauwhata's wattle plantation in a modest beginning of a viticultural station, they too were all non-grafted and so phylloxera-prone.

Tens of thousands of cuttings were distributed from both stations over the next few years but little or no emphasis was put on using grafted stock. Confidence continued to be placed in soil injections and, because New Zealand's widely scattered vineyards did not offer the same scope for cross-infestation as occurred overseas, the department's policy for a time seemed to be successful.

A new spraying machine.

Its report of 1900 said with some smugness: 'It would be tedious to detail the arguments in favour of the carbon bisulphide treatment and those that have been brought forward against it; suffice it to say that events have proved its use in New Zealand to be judicious.' That year a departmental entomologist, T.A. Potter, planted two acres of his own property at Whangarei in ungrafted European vines — which, the *Farmer* remarked, 'seeing that Mr Potter has been busy for a long time inspecting and destroying phylloxera would seem to show he has confidence in the government to eventually stamp out the pest'.

Within a year there were phylloxera outbreaks on a larger scale than ever. Among the vineyards destroyed was the six-acre Kaipara property of W.H. Jackman, planted with Momohaki cuttings and photographed as a model in the department's report of 1899.

An unofficial grape trial in the 1960s by Robert Duncan at Gilligans Gully, Central Otago. Taking up the province's viticultural promise was still years away.

(Dick Scott)

In 1901 Romeo Bragato was invited to return to New Zealand to investigate the industry again. After a five-month tour of the country he diplomatically reported that while the department's efforts were to be commended only the replanting of vineyards on resistant stocks would control phylloxera. He was offered a permanent post as government viticulturist, and addressing a growers' conference after his appointment frankly spelt out the situation. Badly advised growers, he said, had planted vines selected indiscriminately, 'and now they find themselves in possession of stocks perhaps unsuitable to the locality, non-resistant to ordinary diseases, and still less to the attacks of phylloxera'. There was, he added, no cheap substance which, applied to the soil, would absolutely kill the phylloxera without destroying the vine it infected. 'Unless existing vines were promptly replaced by American resistant stocks the vineyards of New Zealand would disappear one by one.'

Thanks to Bragato, the disastrous era of half measures was over.

Six

Romeo Bragato Returns

Romeo Bragato had electrified the country in 1895 with his vision of the prospects for winemaking. The rush to plant vineyards had been called 'grape fever' after that visit, and was so widespread that George Alderton later sourly observed that phylloxera was a good thing, since it stopped more from joining the rush. The Bragato of 1902 had lost none of his capacity to fire enthusiasm.

Te Kauwhata and Arataki

'I am more than ever convinced that wine of very good quality can be produced from New Zealand vineyards,' he said in his first report as head of the newly established Viticultural Division of the Department of Agriculture. 'I have no hesitation whatever in advising growers to embark largely in the industry.'

Bragato's first step was to supply phylloxera-resistant vines. He persuaded a conference of growers 'to strengthen the hands of the department' by resolving that experimental viticultural nurseries be established to supply resistant stocks and to study the needs of different districts.

The vineyard of four acres at Te Kauwhata was expanded to twenty acres as American stocks became available and the original vines were uprooted. In 1903 a second state vineyard, the Arataki Experimental Station, was opened on land purchased from Bernard Chambers at Te Mata, Havelock North, and thirty acres were planted. S.F. Anderson, manager of Greenmeadows Vineyard since

A vine in its fifth year, pruned as recommended by Bragato, and illustrated in his 1895 report.

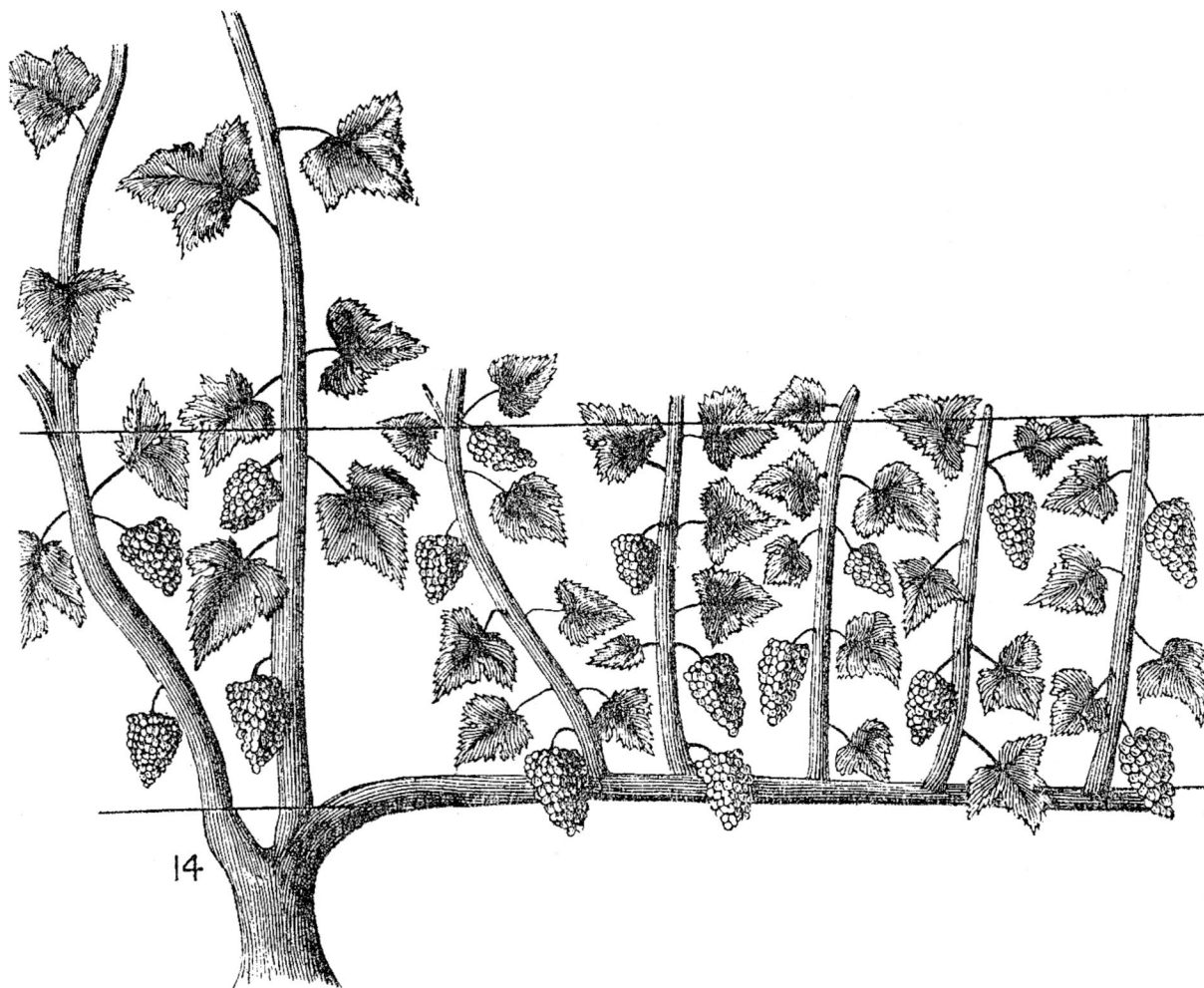

Tiffen's time, was put in charge. (Two years later he was transferred to Te Kauwhata and T.F. Ellis, superintendent of a state viticultural station in New South Wales, was brought over to replace him at Arataki.)

Vines from all over Europe (including the Royal School of Viticulture and Oenology at Conegliano, near Venice, where Bragato had gained his diploma) were imported to test their compatibility with American roots and their performance under New Zealand conditions. Most of the country's vineyards were reconstituted with vines from the two stations. Even Hawkes Bay, which had escaped infestation, changed to grafted stock and Greenmeadows, Te Mata and Frimley between them reached a total of eighty acres under vines. A.J. Vidal, ready for a third attempt after the ill-luck of Wanganui and Palmerston North, bought five quarter-acre sections in Hastings and began growing grapes under glass and outdoors. A racing stable on the property which had housed a prominent jumper called California was converted into a winery and thereafter fortunes changed — Anthony Vidal went on to prosper and California never won another race.

In the north, growers like W.H. Jackman of Whakapirau on the Kaipara painfully started again from scratch and there was an influx of newcomers. Norman May planted nine acres at Hupara in the Bay of Islands and Bray at Swanson, Leeds at Matakana and Carlson and Captain Crapp in the Bay of Plenty were some of the many who tried their hand at winemaking. But the industry's secure establishment was to rest with men who brought skills with them from their homeland.

Assid Abraham Corban, from the wine country of Lebanon, who had been in New Zealand for ten years (broken by a return home to bring out his family) chose this favourable time to enter the wine industry. His Mt Lebanon Vineyard established at Henderson in 1902 with four acres under grapes was to treble in size within ten years — all planted with grafted European varieties or Franco-American hybrids. There were some who persisted with ordinary American vines despite the doubtful winemaking qualities of the Isabella and its New Zealand sport, the Albany Surprise, but in a press interview Corban dismissed their lack of enterprise with the remark, 'Albany Surprise is an ideal grape for the lazy grower.' His much-photographed vineyard and winery were held up as object lessons in what could be done on poor gumland soil.

The Reluctant 'Austrians'

Bragato also welcomed a new group of winemakers first mentioned in an Agricultural Department report of 1896 with a brief note: 'At Pahi (north Kaipara) a number of Austrians are beginning to cultivate the vine on an extensive scale.' After a visit to the Far North in 1904 Bragato reported:

> At the Puhata Settlement, Herekino, a number of Austrian settlers are already beginning to profit by their industry and enterprise. A large area has been planted in vines and small cellars erected, which have been working well during the past year. An excellent wine was produced, and promises well for the future prospects of these useful settlers.

The 'Austrians' were most reluctant Austrians, men from Dalmatia on the Adriatic coast of present-day Croatia who preferred to migrate rather than suffer poverty or serve as conscripts in the Balkan Wars of the Austro-Hungarian Empire. The first group arrived on northern gumfields in the mid-eighties and a decade later more than 500 were digging kauri gum. They worked in large co-operative gangs digging 'on a face', that is turning over all soil above the gum layer in a prodigious effort of pre-mechanised open-cast mining. They were greeted with abuse in some quarters, the *Herald*, no friend of the free-and-easy diggers, calling them in 1893 'the greatest pest of all', but the most a Royal Commission could find that year was that they were 'honest, industrious and frugal'.

Their industry was their undoing. It brought over-production and an 1898 Act excluding aliens from kauri gum reserves was aimed solely at the Dalmatians. This law, and exhaustion of the gum, prompted many to turn to the vinegrowing they had known at home. Wineshops were opened, as many as five on one gumfield. Typically, on the Ahipara field (where almost the first building was a dancehall) wine was sold to the dancers until their cash gave out and then credit was given on a promise to pay in kauri gum chips.

The energy that had gone into digging, now poured into the refractory soil of the north, drew this report from Bragato:

> Among those who are entering largely into grape-growing and winemaking are the Austrian immigrants, who have

'Babich Bros' expands: a winery included in the family's kauri gum enterprise at Waiharara in the Far North.

(Joseph Babich)

formerly confined themselves to gum-digging. Many are now taking up land and planting it with grapes. They spare no pains and exercise the greatest care in the proper preparation of the land prior to planting, and take a pride in keeping the newly planted vineyard clean and well cultivated, with healthy and vigorous vines. Gum-digging provides them with sufficient income to live on while the vines are coming into bearing, when this unsatisfactory occupation can be abandoned and their labour utilized in improving their holdings. In this way many of these men, who were formerly looked at askance and regarded by some as undesirable immigrants, may now be counted as industrious, sober and thrifty settlers, with a permanent attachment to and substantial stake in this country of their adoption.

Three Frankovich brothers at Arkles Bay on the Whangaparaoa Peninsula, forty kilometres north of Auckland, had proved the Dalmatian winemakers' adaptability to New Zealand conditions as early as 1899. A travelling salesman, Ivan Segetin, who that year made the rounds of all his countrymen's settlements in the north, found the Frankovich vineyard the most advanced he had seen. He commented (in an interview fifty years later): 'It can be said they were the first Dalmatians to make a success in the winegrowing industry in New Zealand.' By 1908 the brothers had sixteen acres (six hectares) under vines.

Another early grower with more than a sentimental vine along the fence or a small cask in the kitchen was Andrew Sinkovich, who arrived in New Zealand in 1897, planted an acre at Kerikeri a year later and gave his occupation as winegrower when naturalized in 1900. A father and son, Nicholas and John Silich, winemakers and wine merchants in their own country who had been driven to migrate by the Austrian authorities' policy of importing Italian wines, had established a vineyard at Hukatere in the Far North by 1900. When ten acres of vines in full bearing were later wiped out by phylloxera, however, they had to go back to gum-digging.

John Vella, for more than ten years a fisherman at Paremata, north of Wellington, began a vineyard at Otaki in 1899. Like A.J. Vidal, he found the west coast climate unsuitable and moved near Auckland where he planted six acres at Oratia in 1903. Vella was one of the first growers of consequence in this area (the Marinovich brothers were two others) and, with his seventeen-year-old son Stephen as secretary, took a prominent part in the early Viticultural Association until he despaired of the government's good faith in resisting the prohibitionists and withdrew from the industry. The only Dalmatian from this earliest period to found a vineyard that has survived as a commercial undertaking was Stephen Yelas, who bought gumland at Henderson in 1895, planted grapes in 1902 when the gum ran out, and so established the still-flourishing Pleasant Valley Vineyard.

Emphasis on Quality

Stephen Yelas, founder of Henderson's oldest vineyard. Beginning in 1899, he wrested the seven-acre Pleasant Valley Vineyard from harsh gumland — forty years of heavy toil, not even a horse to lighten the labour.

Instruction in winemaking was as sadly needed as good advice on grape varieties at this time and under Bragato's direction a wine cellar and a laboratory were built at Te Kauwhata. The first 1000 gallons of wine, made in the 1902–1903 seasons, were three reds and a white made from Cabernet Sauvignon, Shiraz (Red Heritage), equal quantities of Pinot Noir and Pinot Meunier and a Verdelho. In 1908 the station was awarded a gold medal by the Franco-British Exhibition in London for a wine 'approaching the Bordeaux clarets in lightness and delicacy' and, although not advertising its products, Te Kauwhata was already selling all the wines it could produce.

In his laboratory Bragato analysed wine samples for growers and tested insecticides. Frequent complaints had been received of sprays that were ineffective or even injurious and he reported, 'I am not surprised that this should be so and I attribute it to the adulterated materials that are often sold.'

Adulterated wines also drew his fire. In 1903 and again in 1904 he called for a law to stop the sale of cheap 'sham wines' which gave unfair competition and brought suspicion on all wines. 'I have found,' he wrote, 'that somehow adulterated wine which is prohibited in the different wine-producing countries of the world finds its way into our colony in considerable quantities, this being made possible by the absence of prohibitive legislation here.'

An Adulteration Bill failed to go through parliament and four years later he was still campaigning:

The production of 'faked' rubbish is still lamentably heavy, and continues to inflict serious injury on the genuine growers.

While the sale of sand and shell as bonedust is punishable with a severe penalty, it is hard to understand why it is permissible to poison invalids and others with some spurious concoction, sold as 'New Zealand wine', in which the grape is a totally foreign body or an unknown quantity.

The Sale of Food and Drugs Act passed in 1908 failed to check abuses and Bragato declared that legislation was more urgently needed than ever to save 'the good name of our local wines'.

Bragato travelled the country advising growers, supervising winemaking, and addressing meetings. He glowed with optimism. Good land for grape culture could be bought for £1 to £5 an acre, the cost of bringing a vineyard to bearing would not exceed £30 an acre, in full production it would yield 400 to 500 gallons of wine an acre ('oftener it runs to 600 or 700') and no grower received less than six shillings a gallon for bulk sales, many as high as ten shillings. Even at 2/6 a gallon the grower would gross £50 to £60 per acre. There were enquiries from London capitalists with £60,000 to invest in New Zealand winemaking, he told the press in 1904, but only the shortage of resistant stocks held them back.

Hothouse grapes under glass could be ripened without difficulty by August or September, he told a growers' conference in 1904. 'It takes the breath away,' said Arch Wilson of Birkenhead, who admitted that the earliest he had marketed his crop was 25 November. In friendly challenge he offered Bragato the use of his glasshouse to prove his words. Bragato accepted, forced the crop with rotted animal manure, and, on the last day of September, the first ripe grapes were sent to market. Altogether 345 pounds of Black Hamburghs were produced from a lean-to vinery of sixty feet by fifteen feet and the first shipment to public auction in Wellington realized the record price of 5/3 a pound.

Bragato's colourful personality helped attract interest in Te Kauwhata's work. Special trains ran to annual field days where two hundred or more growers regularly sat down to lunch in a large marquee erected on the front lawn. His 134-page handbook *Viticulture in New Zealand* was distributed in an edition of 5000 copies.

There was talk of establishing viticultural stations at Whangarei, Kaipara, Hokianga and Tauranga. Bragato selected land at these places where he could experiment with grape varieties for local soils and climate and demonstrate his methods to winemakers too

Inside the cellar at Te Kauwhata government viticultural centre, built by Romeo Bragato in 1903. The hand press mounted on rails and the fermenting vats fed by chute from a floor above were major technological advances for the time.

ROMEO BRAGATO
RETURNS

isolated to journey to Te Kauwhata.[1] But at this point the official blight that hovered over his schemes now began to fall in earnest. The new stations failed to materialize and the vineyard areas at Te Kauwhata and Arataki were themselves restricted.

Bragato had suffered much frustration. He had complained of having to run the Viticultural Division without proper clerical assistance; a proposal that accommodation be provided for cadets to be trained as managers of vineyards and wine cellars, 'positions which I am convinced will soon be numerous', was rejected as often as it was presented; repeated requests for cellar accommodation ('at present the whole of the wine is injudiciously stored in the fermenting-house') were declined with the result that plans to 'publicly demonstrate that a high-class champagne can be produced here at low cost' had to be abandoned.

Perhaps Bragato made too many suggestions. He wanted a lecture hall and small agricultural museum at Te Kauwhata, too, and the issue of fortnightly bulletins and liaison with teachers and schools. Perhaps it was just the rust of official machinery that thwarted him or even lingering resentment at his spectacular reversal of departmental policy on phylloxera. In any case something worse than phylloxera was now making itself felt — prohibition — and Bragato was one of its first casualties.

Worse than Phylloxera

Year by year the strength of the prohibitionists had been growing. In 1905, when they succeeded in adding their first North Island dry district (Grey Lynn) to the five no-licence areas won in the South Island, Bragato reported that vignerons felt their occupation to be a precarious one, 'liable at any general election to be crippled by the work of the Prohibitionist Party'. But ever-optimistic, he had a solution — there would still remain 'a profitable market, at present untouched, in the manufacture of unfermented grape-juice'. Growers were unpersuaded and vineyard plantings declined.

---

1. Ironically, the man who wanted better sites has sometimes been blamed for the unsatisfactory choice of Te Kauwhata. Visiting wine expert André Simon was told in 1964 that Bragato had selected the place for no better reason than that the landscape reminded him of Italy. In fact, the Department of Agriculture began planting 1800 acres in wattle, eucalyptus and oak trees there in 1887, and ten years later the pomologist W.J. Palmer planted the first vines. It was then called the Waerenga Vineyard.

To accelerate the downward trend the government chose this moment to lift restrictions on imports of Australian table grapes, and the permanent head of the Agriculture Department reflected the official attitude by complacently noting that while those who had erected large greenhouses would suffer, 'the matter will, however, probably resolve itself into a question of the greatest good for the greatest number'.[2]

Two years later when Bragato wrote of 'the rapid strides the industry is making' and its 'extremely promising future' the permanent head of his department, in a preface to the same report, permitted himself the dry understatement that wine grape plantings showed no great increase, laconically adding: 'It is doubtful whether the cultivation of this class of grape will receive much attention in the near future.'

In 1908 control of Te Kauwhata and Arataki viticultural stations was transferred from Romeo Bragato to the Livestock and Agriculture Division and Bragato was left to run the Viticultural Division single-handed. The following year he retired, his division was disbanded and Te Kauwhata manager S.F. Anderson was appointed vine and wine instructor under the control of the Orchards, Gardens and Apiaries Division. Shortly afterwards Bragato left the country for Canada where he ended his life by leaping from an upper-storey window following a crisis in his domestic affairs.

---

2. Although there was overproduction of wine in Australia where grape prices dropped as low as twenty shillings a ton, the matter was resolved by the Australians being driven from the market. Thanks to a mutation in an Albany, Auckland orchard, some years before, New Zealand table grapes offered at fifty per cent higher prices sold out while the imports rotted. In the mid-nineties orchardist George Pannell noticed one of his Isabella vines had thrown up three particularly strong canes, quite distinct from the rest with a larger, less indented leaf and much larger, superior fruit. Besieged for cuttings, after his first crop reached the market in 1897 he refused to supply any and rival growers broke in and helped themselves. The vine, named Albany Surprise, was distributed by a nurseryman the following year and, despite departmental condemnation, swiftly became the most widely grown table variety in New Zealand. It makes poor wine, however, unless the fruit is dead ripe.

Assid Abraham Corban defends young vines from the birds.

A new generation of Corbans beneath loaded vines at Mt Lebanon Vineyards and a granddaughter beside grapes on their way to the crusher.

Assid Corban and his son Wadier with their new crusher.

OPPOSITE
Najib and Annis drive off under their father's eye with a day's pickings.

Khaleel Corban and sisters Zarefy and Annisie take Depression-time cheer to Taranaki.

OPPOSITE
Wadier Assid Corban presides over a richly fermenting vat.

OVERLEAF
A monument to prohibition's absurdities, the little building (right) is a depot where it was legal for A.A. Corban & Sons to sell their wines when it was illegal to do so from the cellars (left) where they were made. For ten years after 1908 the railway was the boundary between 'wet' and 'dry' electorates. The depot, preserved as a part of history, still stands alongside Great North Road, Henderson.

OVERLEAF BELOW
Counter-attacking the prohibitionists before a national poll in 1919, Corbans displays such slogans as 'You Fought for Liberty — Vote for It' at the Auckland Spring Show.

Thirty Lean Years

Prohibition Threat

The president of New Zealand's first Temperance Society was a winemaker. This was James Busby and the society, formed in the Bay of Islands in 1836, saw no inconsistency in electing such a man to its head. In fact, Busby's winemaking was part of his interest in temperance. 'The settler soaks over his keg of rum, till he has drained it to the dregs, regardless of the squalid wretchedness of his family,' Busby once wrote. 'If the bodily strength were daily renewed, after labour, by the use of a liquor which could be pretty freely indulged in, without intoxication, the same longing for stronger drink would not be felt.' That liquor was wine, diluted with water 'as used by the lower orders in Europe', and Busby contrasted 'the stupefying effects of the muddling ale' and 'the liquid fire' of spirits with such a drink — 'a light and exhilarating beverage, calculated to cheer the heart and to elevate the spirits without confusing the understanding'.

Busby's views were to be dramatically confirmed when phylloxera swept through Europe bringing alcoholism to the 'lower orders' as they met the wine famine by using cheap spirits (the 'higher orders' turned from brandy to whisky and their incidence of alcoholism was unchanged), but the later prohibition movement had no room for the lessons of history or the liberal compromise of its Bay of Islands forerunners. All wine was 'demon drink' to be banished along with the rest — banished even from the Bible by tremendous theses which proved to their authors' satisfaction that the wine of the scriptures was not wine at all but unfermented grape juice.

In 1908 the prohibitionists registered their first victory in wine districts when Masterton and Eden (an Auckland electorate including part of Henderson) voted no-licence. After the poll a Masterton winemaker, W.G. Lamb, was prosecuted for selling directly from his Tararua Vineyard. The magistrate dismissed the charge and the police appealed. The chief justice, Sir Robert Stout, a well-known prohibitionist, upheld the prosecution. Lamb's 7000 Pinot Noir vines, planted in 1897 and used to make claret, hock and a sweet red wine, were destroyed.

Notorious for extreme blue-ribbon views ('I will have no parley or truce with the sale of poison,' he said at this time when asked by English journalist, W.T. Stead, if he would support state control of liquor), Stout did not attempt to conceal his bias in court. He declared that not only could a winemaker not sell wine but also, in his opinion, he could not even make wine in a no-licence area. This gratuitous extension of the law drew a statement from the Crown Law Office published in the *Journal of Agriculture*. Quoting Stout's judgement, it confirmed that a winemaker could neither sell wine nor accept orders to sell within a no-licence district. It went on:

There is nothing, however, to prevent such a person manufacturing wine from grapes grown in his vineyard in a

CRISIS IN THE WINE INDUSTRY

A pamphlet presenting the wine-growers' case, written by A.R.D. Fairburn and printed at the Pelorus Press by Robert Lowry.

no-license district; and there is nothing to prevent him establishing a depot or cellars anywhere outside the boundaries of the no-license district, and removing all wine manufactured to that depot. If he does that he can sell his wine from that depot to customers, whether they reside in a no-license or in a license district.

Henderson winemakers acted on this advice. Depots were erected in the 'wet' half of their district and local sales continued. In one case where a railway line formed both the frontage to a property and the boundary line between electorates, land was bought on the 'wet' side of the line, a depot was built a chain away from the 'dry' cellars — and the law was satisfied.

While the growers were forced into senseless expense by the prohibitionists, their livelihood was attacked from other quarters. In 1908 the government amended the Distilling Act to raise from two acres to five the minimum area before a still was permitted. Since each vineyard was allowed to distil only its own spirit, small growers deprived of licences were prevented from combining their acreage to license a co-operative still. They had to buy imported brandy.

There was discrimination in other ways. Hawkes Bay winemakers pointed out that fruitgrowing neighbours had their cases returned by rail free of charge while they had to pay for the return of empty containers. Unlike other industries, winemakers had to pay heavy duties on imported materials. To make it worse they had to compete with cheap South African wine enjoying a preferential tariff. The duty on Australian wine of five shillings a gallon was fair protection to local growers, the *Farmer* declared in a 1911 editorial, but 'the fact that South African wines (the product of cheap coloured labour) should be allowed to be imported, with only 2/- per gallon duty, seems an extraordinary anomaly, considering the professed Liberal and Labour principles of the present government'. The duty was not raised for ten years, and then to 4/6.

Where the North Auckland Vinegrowers' Association had in 1903 pressed for local wine to be sold in restaurants, now its successor, the New Zealand Viticultural Association, had to fight to sell wine anywhere. In 1912 the national association petitioned the prime minister 'to save this fast decaying industry by initiating such legislation as will restore confidence among those who, after long years of waiting have almost lost confidence in the justice of the government'. The petitioners declared that through harsh laws and 'withdrawal of government support and encouragement that had been promised, a great industry had been practically ruined'.

The officers of the association were: president, Captain C.A. Young; secretary, Stephen Vella; treasurer, E.P. Seymour; committee, John Vella, A.A. Corban, Stephen Kokich, Fabian Petrie, H. Mertz and Lawrence Marinovich. These were men of some substance but no concessions were forthcoming from politicians walking a razor edge between prohibitionists' votes and financial inducements from the liquor trade.

Still fighting the adulteration battle taken up by Bragato, the association asked that winemakers be licensed and that inspectors be appointed to test wines for 'deleterious additions'. Yet two years later, when the 1914 Licensing Amendment Act introduced licences for the first time, no credit was given the association for having pressed for control of the industry. Prime minister W.F. Massey instead made a sweeping attack on Dalmatian winemakers, using as a basis the report of a kauri gum industry committee that had criticised the way wineshops on the gumfields were conducted.

'Austrian wine' had caused loss of life and it would be 'put down with very drastic measures', Massey told the House. His description was lurid, if imprecise:

> I do not know whether the name is a misnomer or not; but it is a liquor that is sold in the district north of Auckland. I have never seen the stuff, but I believe it to be one of the vilest decoctions which can possibly be imagined. I do not know what its ingredients are, but I have come across people who have seen the effect of the use of Austrian wine as a beverage, and from what I learned it is a degrading, demoralizing and sometimes maddening drink to many people who use it . . . [1]

Not surprisingly, when the war came, the Massey Government could not distinguish between foe and friend and many Dalmatians, inflexibly defined as Austrian enemy aliens, were taken from their homes and sent to work-camps. The war also gave new opportunities to the prohibitionists. Their campaigning brought the country to the brink of national prohibition: only the soldiers' votes saved the wine industry from extinction without compensation.

Not even the laborious depot arrangement at Henderson could go undisturbed. In 1918 Eden boundaries were changed and all of Henderson was brought into the no-licence area. Now the depots were unusable.

In 1919 there was a glimmer of light when a parliamentary select committee appointed to encourage local industry accepted a strong case presented by the Viticultural Association for special consideration of the wine industry. The committee reported:

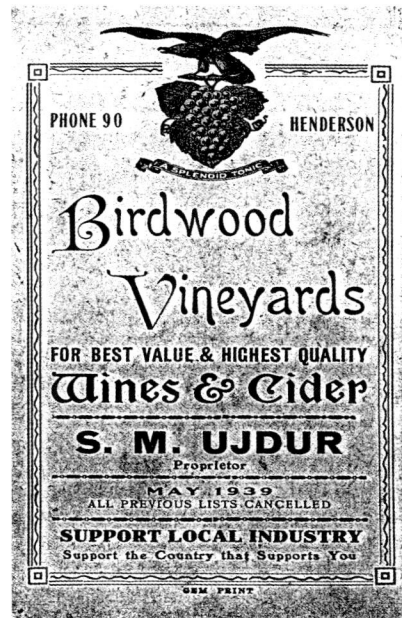

Birdwood Vineyards, founded in 1915, was one of the country's leading producers in the first half of the twentieth century.

---

1. Some Dalmatians were undoubtedly producing 'plonk' — but they had no monopoly in this respect. And for all Massey's fury the legislation as it finally emerged merely required that licences be granted to persons of good character, whether they were good winemakers or not. In 1915, thirty-five were issued.

A considerable amount of capital has been invested in the establishment of vineyards as well as in the requisite and costly plants for the manufacture and storage of wines. Your committee has taken evidence from vignerons and others, with the result that it has come to the conclusion that legislation should be provided to remove the industry from the present uncertainty and possible danger of being destroyed by votes cast on the question of prohibition of the liquor trade. In a portion of Canada which is now under prohibition this principle has been adopted and in Australia it is proposed to make a similar provision. Without in any way desiring to raise the debatable question of liquor or no liquor, your committee is of the opinion that the manufacture of wines of good quality and unfortified should not be interfered with.

Here was the first breath of sanity in decades, but no action followed. The only move made by the first post-war government was backwards, to alter the 1881 legislation by which winebar licences were granted. An amendment to the Licensing Act in 1920 sealed off this form of sale by providing that no further licences could be issued.

To sell their product it was necessary for the growers to find another gap in the legal thickets that smothered them. The bizarre situation that continued was described in 1925 in a student thesis by a winegrower's son (Dr Corban Assid Corban) who wrote:

The legal complications distorted the anomalies. A maker could not supply any customer in the Eden district, although it was legal for a maker in another district to do so . . . Eden customers could get their wine from Hawkes Bay, but not from makers in their own locality. Could anything be more ridiculous? The legal tangle further prevented a maker from supplying at two sources. If he erected a depot elsewhere to assist local customers, wines intended for wet areas throughout the whole Dominion would all have to pass from that site. In one instance it was decided to sever the connection of several hundred customers and refund a considerable sum that had accompanied wine orders. For several years these folk were deprived of the ability to get any satisfaction, but recently some attempt was made in one

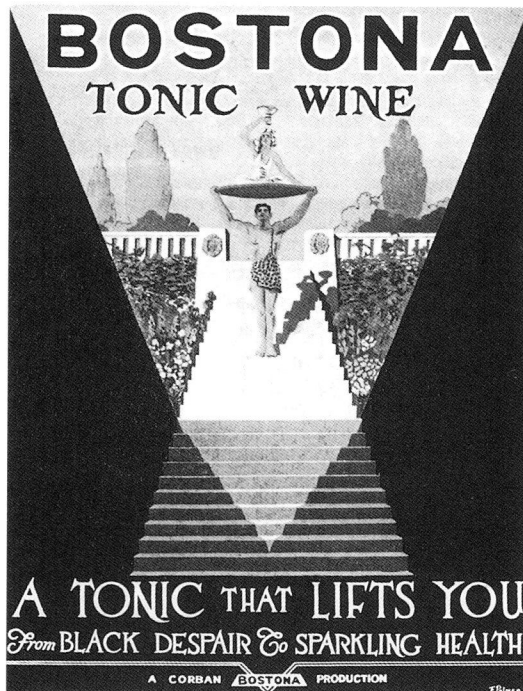

BOSTONA
TONIC WINE

A TONIC THAT LIFTS YOU
From BLACK DESPAIR & SPARKLING HEALTH

A CORBAN BOSTONA PRODUCTION

One way to meet Depression woes and circumvent the prohibitionists: a tonic wine showcard for chemist shop windows.

instance to solve the difficulty by a costly and quixotic method which the anomalous law justifies. The honest neighbour can now get his case from a person outside the electorate, the said person purchasing and stocking considerable quantities of cased wines, and reselling them to the Eden customers in the usual way, since he is not in the same electoral district. The Clerk of Court is notified as usual. Considering that avoidable freights have to be paid both ways, to and from the premises of this independent salesman, and that commissions, higher prices, and delays must necessarily be accompanying features, it will be seen what ample scope there is for rectifying a notoriously anomalous legal absurdity.

The scope for remedying legal absurdities was to yet further widen. In 1924 the first regulations for the control of winemaking were issued under the 1908 Sale of Food and Drugs Act. Three of them, if enforced, would have made winemaking virtually impossible.[2]

2. The addition of water, often necessary to reduce acidity, was prohibited; only wine spirits could be used for fortifying although growers with under five acres were prevented from having a still or buying from others; wine could be made from grapes only, making all fruit and citrus wines illegal.

Prosecutions brought by the police on behalf of the Health Department in 1927 served only to underline the farce. Refusing to convict a winemaker for fortifying with foreign brandy supplied for the purpose by Customs at a reduced duty, the magistrate said that one government department was prosecuting winemakers for what another government department approved.

A joyless chapter ends with the trials of the winemaker drowned by the woes of the nation. Now the great depression settled over the country and as the economy axe chopped blindly at pensions, hospitals, schools and public works what cry could be heard when it fell on a viticultural station? In 1933 Te Kauwhata was put up for public auction. There were no bidders.

OPPOSITE

'A drink of wine is like a garden of flowers … it is not only a food, but an art in life … it is the spirit of companionship between man and man.' So Paul Groshek, individualist and visionary, told parliament in one of his petitions for reform of the laws governing the wine industry. He was photographed at the entrance to his maze of underground cellars not long before death ended his one-man crusade in 1963.

(ROD HARVEY)

Vine Brkan and Peter Popovich whirl in the kola at the Auckland Connoisseurs' Club's first annual vintage celebration, Redwood Park, Swanson, 1966. Two special trains carried 1250 members to all-day festivities. The number attending was soon to double.

(MARTI FRIEDLANDER)

The enthusiasm of spirited dancers was catching on a sunny day and wine-enthused members soon joined in.
(MARTI FRIEDLANDER)

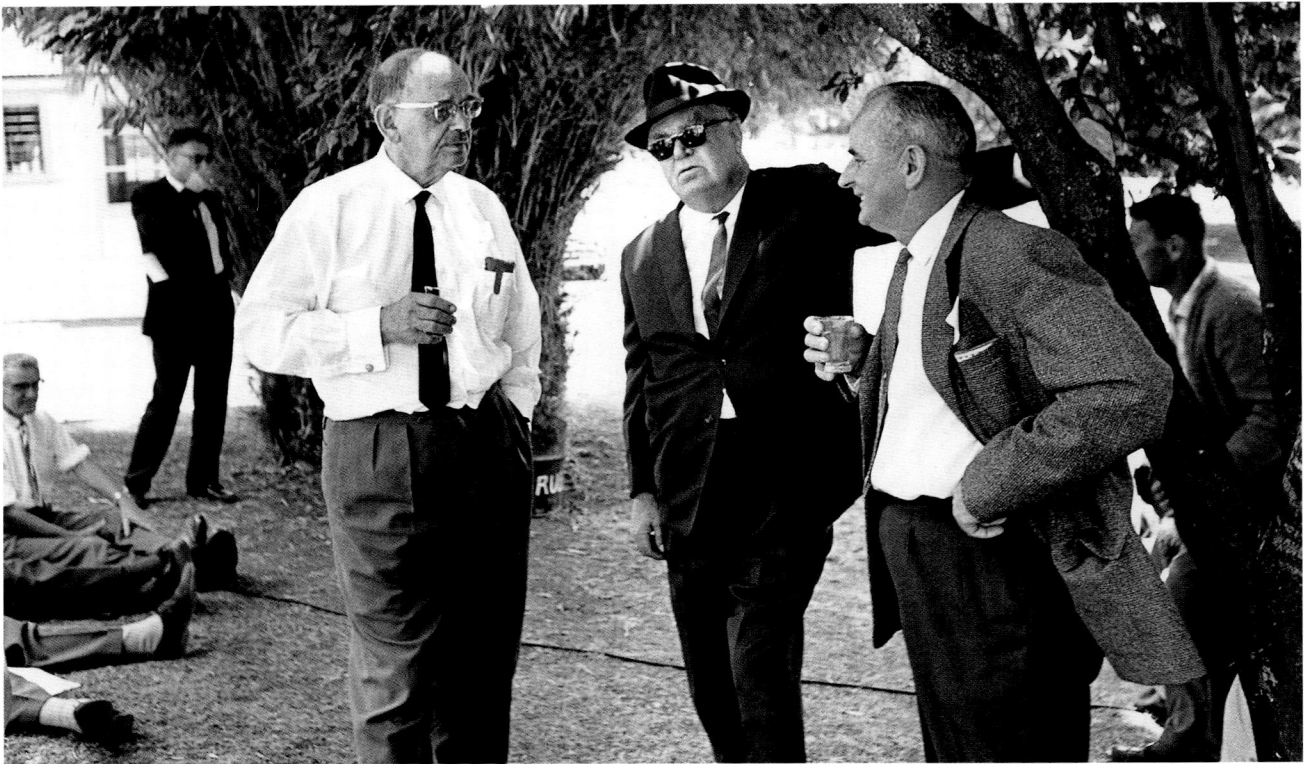

Sir Douglas Robb, Sir Leslie Munro, MP, and D.J. Carter, MP, join winemakers at Te Kauwhata Research Station's annual field day in 1967.

Dr Jack Perle, Ruakura research scientist, lectures at the 1967 Te Kauwhata field day.

(Marti Friedlander photographs)

Alister McKissock, Te Kauwhata research officer, and Dr Jack Perle, his Ruakura counterpart, make a field-day evaluation.

(Marti Friedlander)

The lush sub-tropical setting of Western Vineyards, Henderson Valley. In the visitors' book, wine authority André Simon wrote: 'I have never seen a more picturesque vineyard anywhere but in Tuscany.'

André Simon speaks at the Viticultural Association's field day at Panorama Vineyards during his 1964 tour. The progress of a young country's winemakers amazed him.

(GRAHAM MCKECHNIE, *AUCKLAND STAR*)

Viggo Dufresne, one of only two licensed grape winemakers in the South Island in 1968, tends his Ruby Bay vines where Tasman rollers have left deep shoals of water-worn gravel.

(MARTI FRIEDLANDER)

Changing the face of a province, Montana introduces large-scale planting to Marlborough in 1973 with vines running to the hills in rows almost a kilometre long. At the far end a worker with telescopic sights is lining up with the flag to ensure the rows run straight.

Judge David Beattie (former Montana chairman and later governor-general) plants the company's first Marlborough vine. Mate Yukich and managing director Frank Yukich, with Ronald Davison QC, the new chairman (later the chief justice) look on. In ten years Montana had already increased annual production from 30,000 gallons to over a million gallons.

Heavy emphasis from Frank Yukich for a brewery's wine and spirit manager, Devon Hern. The liquor trade's shutting out of New Zealand wines was coming to an end.
(IVAN PEACE, *WINE REVIEW*)

Eight

Salute the Survivors

Tested By
Adversity

All over the world, Roger Dion, a French geographer, has pointed out, customs and beliefs have had more influence than climate on the distribution of vineyards. Exceeding even the vine in tenacity were the winemakers who took root in New Zealand opposed not by climate but by customs and beliefs. After all the blights, manmade and natural, that they had overcome, a depression could not be expected to subdue them.

At Gisborne, where the unemployed staged a hunger march to Wellington, a German winemaker, Friedrich Wohnsiedler, found a market for wines he had to bring over fourteen kilometres by horse and cart from a vineyard at Waihirere. By 1935 he had scraped enough savings to buy a motor car for his deliveries. The vineyard had been established in 1921 after First World War patriots had totally wrecked his pork butchery and delicatessen in Gisborne's main street — a nationwide renaming of German sausage as Belgian sausage not having satisfied their loyal feelings. After more than twenty years in New Zealand, Wohnsiedler had decided to make a new start as a winemaker. With the help of Poverty Bay's first winemaker since Father Lampila, Peter Guschka, an Austrian blacksmith at Manutuke who ran a vineyard and cellar as a sideline, he laid the foundations of Waihirere Wines Ltd, which by the 1960s was producing 95,000 gallons a year and was steadily expanding.

Typical of models still in use during the Depression, this wine press was imported from France a century ago by John Vella for his Oratia vineyard. Tony Ivicevich of Panorama Vineyards, who bought it in 1935, demonstrates the ratchet action of the handle.

From Henderson, Dalmatian winemakers walked seven or eight kilometres to the station along dirt roads, caught a train to an Auckland suburb, and canvassed door-to-door with a suitcase of samples. For men like Joe Babich who had crushed grapes with a manuka stick, tramped out the juice in a barrel with his bare feet and, as a boy on Far North gumfields, had ridden sixty-five kilometres to a customer with a sack of half-a-dozen port wine each side of the saddle and then sixty-five kilometres back with £1 to show for his journey, the labour of finding a depression-time householder with money to spend was no special hardship.

In fact, wine offered some cheer in these bleak days and sales even increased. One Dalmatian pioneer, Joseph Balich, whose Golden Sunset Vineyard was established in 1912 — planted by candlelight at night after a day's work for A.A. Corban — developed such a round of regular customers that he could afford a Model T van. And, afford it or not, he even helped his countrymen to establish vineyards all over Henderson by giving bank guarantees and interest-free loans — not to speak of countless wedding receptions at his home for those starting off a typical Dalmatian working partnership.[1]

In Hawkes Bay, Tom McDonald's five acres of vines purchased in 1927 were increased by seven acres in 1934 but chill winds from the economic freeze-up had whistled through his earth-floor cellar. Only as he sold wine could he buy materials to make more wine. The Averill brothers at Henderson took out a wine licence in 1928 to help in the struggle to make a living from their orchard. (Founded within a year of each other in districts 480 kilometres apart, both vineyards were to follow a remarkably parallel course in later years. When war conditions and import control first turned brewery interests to the New Zealand wine industry for supplies, Averills signed a long-term contract to supply Dominion Breweries with their total output, thereafter marketed under the Shepherd label, and McDonald Wines amalgamated with Ballins. Then, in

---

1. When Joseph Balich gave a loan there was no lawyer or written agreement and, because he wished to avoid embarrassing those he helped, there were no witnesses either. One beneficiary told the author that Joseph Balich visited his struggling vineyard and suggested improvements. Told this would cost money, Balich tapped his pocket and said: 'That's no trouble. It's here.' He gave a £500 loan without making any arrangements for repayment. When Balich died, £150 still owing was taken to the family. They had no record of the transaction and said: 'Take £50 of it back for your honesty.'

1962, McWilliams Wines of Australia took over McDonalds and the following year Penfolds Wines crossed the Tasman to buy out Averills.)

In 1932 the depression government imposed a five per cent sales tax on New Zealand wine. That year Robert Bird, founder of Glenvale Vineyard, began tunnelling into a Bayview hillside to make a cellar, and the same year nineteen-year-old Dudley Russell established Western Vineyards up the Henderson Valley. A winemaker, like a vine, will establish in any conditions.

While the vineyards of the nineteenth century had died with their founders, some of those from the first years of the 1900s were surviving into the second and third generation: Anthony Vidal of Hastings, Dalmatians such as Stephan Yelas, and A.A. Corban — their labours were enduring where all others had failed.

Throughout years of prohibition and depression the Corban business never ceased to grow. Uncertainty as to the future meant that makeshift additions took the place of new buildings; a great winery 'just grew' from a cottage, levered up inch by inch with a kauri beam while a cellar was excavated underneath. Simple hand-machinery became more complex. In 1916 the first motor arrived, a 1½-horsepower oil engine used to pump water, operate spraying equipment and turn the grape-crusher. By 1927 a wineshop licence at Hawera was taken over and in 1934 the wine and spirit wholesaler's licence held by the Colonial Wine and Spirit Co. (an offshoot of Wendel's wineshop) was purchased.

As early as 1913, Corbans had won two gold and two silver medals for four entries of port, sherry, claret and a sweet red wine in competition with overseas entrants at Auckland, and at the 1925 South Seas Exhibition, Dunedin, Corbans' port again won a gold medal (judging was done at Adelaide) and the sherry was placed second to an entry from Spain. Apart from a brief moment at this exhibition when the governor, Sir Charles Ferguson, asked to taste the gold medal port and was mistakenly given coloured water off a display stand, the Corban name had already secured a firm international reputation for New Zealand wine.

Through the twenties and early thirties the industry was well served by the Department of Agriculture's vine and wine instructor, Charles Woodfin. An Englishman with a passion for viticulture, a unique palate, remarkable memory for wines, and a command of half-a-dozen languages — including Arabic, to the delight of A.A.

Charles Woodfin, a popular vine and wine instructor.

Corban — Woodfin had resigned from the Guards to act as private secretary to a rich English traveller. Before coming to this country he had for a time owned a small Bordeaux vineyard. He was popular with Dalmatian growers, publishing a paper in 1931 on the green method of grafting they had introduced into New Zealand. On leaving the department at the height of the depression he lived in a small bachelor's cottage at Taradale, giving local growers the benefit of his advice even in retirement. Government disinterest was partly counteracted at a difficult time by the enthusiasm of Charles Woodfin.

Labour's False Start

Official encouragement, withdrawn from the industry for thirty years, was restored with the return of a Labour administration in 1935. Te Kauwhata was rehabilitated, given funds to expand its work and install better machinery and equipment, and a new vine and wine instructor, B.W. Lindeman, an Australian from a well-known winemaking family, was appointed.

Government policy of restrictions on imports provided the industry with the opportunity it had waited so long to receive. The liquor trade, which had always excluded the local product in favour of higher-profit imported wines, was forced to offer customers a choice of home-grown and overseas wines — a lowering of barriers reinforced by an unwritten decision of the Industries and Commerce Department that wholesale merchants had to purchase two gallons of New Zealand wine for every gallon received on an import licence.

For a time imports of wine were cut by half and in 1938 the duty on those allowed in was raised to 8/3 a gallon. It was now possible for New Zealand ports to compete in price with the cheap Australian ports that had dominated the market.

Assured in 1939 by government spokesmen at conferences in Wellington that vineyard expansion was in the national interest, winegrowers set in train the costly, slow-maturing process of increasing wine production.

It was not only the unavoidable effects of the war that upset these plans. In 1940 sales tax on New Zealand wine was increased to ten per cent and two years later it soared to forty per cent — twice as much as was imposed on other goods. A case of cheap wine selling at thirty shillings had to carry an additional twelve shillings tax; best quality wine, at 105 shillings a case, paid an additional forty-two shillings tax. Not till 1949, four years after the war ended, were these taxes reduced to the same twenty per cent that other manufacturers paid. At the same time, despite wine-growers' heavy increases in production based on the assurances given in 1939, imports were doubled during some war years and then trebled when the war ended. The minister of customs, Walter Nash, 'is rapidly qualifying for the position of patron saint of the Australian winegrowers — rather, shall we say, of the large commercial interests that handle Australian wines,' commented A.R.D. Fairburn in a pamphlet written for the New Zealand industry.

The Department of Agriculture had not helped to restore confidence in the government during the war years. Regulations drawn up at one stage caused much resentment — one would have denied stills to growers with less than twenty-five acres (ten hectares) of grapes in full bearing — and the New Zealand Viticultural Association complained, in the words of the 1946 Royal Commission on Licensing, that they were 'designed only in the interests of the large growers and were intended to put the small growers out of business. They complained also that they had not been assisted with advice by the new vine and wine instructor.'

Standards of hygiene and methods of manufacture undoubtedly could have been improved in many wineries bent only on supplying wine in quantity to American servicemen, but the commission noted that 'for the conditions which existed the department and the other inspecting authorities do not appear to be free from blame. The visits of inspection seem to have been very infrequent.'

The commission also sympathetically noted the small winemakers' complaint that an 'inequitable and unsatisfactory' distribution of rationed sugar had been made on the advice of the department's instructor. This favoured large concerns since sugar was allocated according to acreage without reference to yield per acre. 'It was admitted by the department's representative that a better system for the allocation of sugar should be adopted.'

Grapes with a natural sugar content of eighteen per cent can be grown without difficulty in New Zealand — in Australia grape-sugar content generally ranges between seventeen per cent and

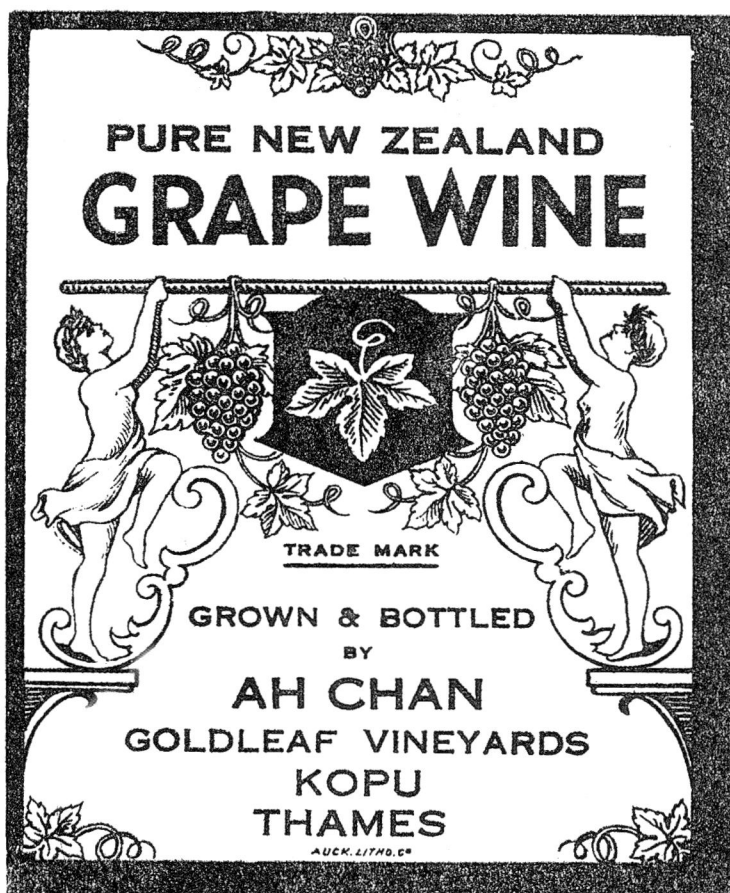

PURE NEW ZEALAND
GRAPE WINE

TRADE MARK

GROWN & BOTTLED
BY
AH CHAN
GOLDLEAF VINEYARDS
KOPU
THAMES

AUCK. LITHO. C°

The Goldleaf Vineyards, established at Thames in 1925 with three acres in grapes, produced 1000 gallons of wine a year for twenty-five years. Sold in 1950 and renamed the Totara Vineyard, it is still operated by a Chinese family. The founder, Joe Ah Chan, was said to be the only Chinese winemaker in the southern hemisphere.

twenty-nine per cent — but, as in European or American vineyards, this amount can fall, especially in a poor season, and must be supplemented by other means.

The addition of cane sugar in quantities of up to two or three pounds to the gallon of grape juice for sweet wines and a half-pound for table wines has long been New Zealand practice. As early as 1895 the winemaker at Tiffen's Greenmeadows Vineyard, Sidney Anderson, noted in his diary: 'Steinmetz told me today that the Mission people added cane sugar to all their wines to bring them up to 25 per cent by the saccharometer. That is any that were under 20 per cent naturally.'

Government regulations, as in Europe or the United States, specify maximum quantities of cane sugar that may be added. (While the New Zealand allowance is comparatively high, few were prepared for the bombshell cast at the 1946 Royal Commission hearing when McWilliams Wines of Australia called for legislation prohibiting the use of sugar altogether. Later, the upper limit of two pounds of sugar per gallon of juice was actually raised.)

A clash of interest between large and small growers led most of the former to break away from the Viticultural Association in 1943 when they formed the New Zealand Wine Council. But a continuing Australian threat temporarily brought the two organisations and the Hawkes Bay Winemakers' Association together in 1948 to form the Wine Manufacturers' Federation of New Zealand. Outside this grouping yet another splinter group was led by Paul Groshek, a winemaker with pronounced and highly individual views, who founded the N.Z. Grape Producers' and Wine Manufacturers' Association (Inc.). A Yugoslav miner who had worked coal in the US and Africa before coming to the West Coast and Waikato mines, Groshek planted a two-acre vineyard at Henderson during the depression, making a cellar by sinking an underground shaft into a hillside. If his petitions to parliament sometimes made orthodox industry spokesmen wince, not the least of their merits was their vivid phrasing. [2]

In 1948 A.R.D. Fairburn gave the background to the industry's fears:

In 1944 it was known that a £50,000 company, an off-shoot of one of the biggest wine companies in Australia, had been registered in New Zealand, with most of its share-capital held in Australia. The purpose of this new organisation, it was gathered, was to import Australian wines into New Zealand, and to grow wine in this country as well. By judicious blending of Australian wine (high in saccharose and alcoholic content) with New Zealand unfortified wine, a commercial product could no doubt be put on the market that would

---

2. 'The wine industry does not start with a £1000 still and 10 tons of grapes, it starts with 10 lbs of grapes and a bucket,' he wrote when the Agriculture Department proposed a three-acre minimum on the size of vineyards. 'We ask for liberty for young New Zealanders to till the soil as they wish.' Some of his wines were named after New Zealand volcanoes — Tongariro Sherry, Ngauruhoe Sparkling Wine, for example — not good public relations, perhaps, in view of the explosive product from some small vineyards the department wished to close down. On the liquor trade boycott of local wines he commented: 'If Danish butter were selling in New Zealand at 15/- per lb, and no grocery shops were handling New Zealand butter, New Zealand dairy farmers would send the government through the vents of Mt. Ngauruhoe, yet that is how the wine industry is being treated.' His evidence to the 1957 select committee concluded:

A glass of wine, good luck to you;
Produce and make, give all good that's mine,
Nothing with us can take in passing across the line.

satisfy the chief demands of the New Zealand public — high alcoholic content, and a high degree of sweetness. If, at the same time, New Zealand winegrowers were compelled by legislation to refrain from using cane-sugar, and from fortifying their product with brandy beyond a certain small limit, the new company would be in a uniquely advantageous position. The local growers would probably be compelled to sell most of their wine to it for blending purposes (at reduced prices, of course).

In the event, after McWilliams Wines of Australia established vineyards in Hawkes Bay with Edward Cullen, the minister of agriculture, planting the first vines in 1947 and B.W. Lindeman, the department's former instructor, taking the post of production manager, none of the dire predictions came true. But on the long record of successive governments' breaches of faith with the industry, could winemakers be blamed for having believed that any duplicity was possible?

Unable to resolve the conflicting evidence put before it, the 1946 Royal Commission had recommended that the government employ an expert, independent of all interests in the country, to make a survey of the wine industry. He should come from a wine country with a climate similar to New Zealand's, it was suggested, perhaps from one of the universities in the north-eastern states of the USA.

The scope for co-operative manufacture of wine, commercial prospects for brandy making, the best site for a government winery or wineries — these would be some of his positive enquiries. He would also investigate the use of cane sugar, report on the blending of imported wines with the New Zealand product, and advise whether a Wine Advisory Board should replace Department of Agriculture control.

Meanwhile, immediate reforms recommended by the commission included tariff and tax adjustments to encourage the production of quality light wines, the sale of wine in restaurants, and easing of restrictions on existing wineshops and authorizing of depots in no-licence areas.

In a brave new post-war world here was a government's opportunity for action. But the spirit of enquiry and reform died with the commission, embalmed in a 450-page printed report on the licensing laws it had taken nineteen months and 7824 pages of typed evidence to produce. A strong recommendation by the chairman, Sir David Smith, a Supreme Court judge, together with a majority of the commission, that a public corporation take over the breweries had left the government with no stomach to heed what the twenty-five page section on the wine industry might say.

In 1948 an amendment to the Licensing Act extended the scope of wholesale, charter and hotel licences — but not of wine licences. A Licensing Control Commission was also set up to investigate the licensing laws and recommend reforms. Winegrowers appeared before the new body at the first hearing in Auckland in 1951 — and found that it had no power to include their evidence in its deliberations.

There was a different government by now, but no difference in attitude: three years later the industry was still pressing for the Licensing Control Commission to be given power to grant wine licences. In written submissions to the minister of justice, the Winemakers' Federation asked these three questions:

Labels from the vineyard of Paul Groshek, the eloquent advocate for a liberalised liquor regime.

(1) If the government recognises Te Kauwhata as an essential unit in building up further supplies of quality wines in New Zealand . . . why then does the government not give the wine industry adequate facilities for the distribution of these wines?

(2) Is it not reasonable for the New Zealand wine industry to expect similar consideration and recognition as is accorded to other primary industries in New Zealand, especially in view of the fact that it provides close land settlement on small acreages, and full employment for complete families and others?

(3) Why should the public be restricted to the purchase of wines in quantities of 2 gallons or more, except through hotels, which many people do not care to patronise?

Simple questions like these remained unanswered although the twentieth century was more than half gone. And Paul Groshek, who petitioned parliament at this time with less rein on his indignation, was clearly an unreasonable man to ask why there could not be wineshops, under licensing trust control, in any town with a population of a thousand or more, 'in our humble vision, an improvement on our present degrading drinking habits'.

Groshek's petition, printed by Robert Lowry at the Pilgrim Press, gave this alternative:

The wineshops would open for twelve hours, from 11 a.m. to 11 p.m., and would be required to provide light meals at any time during open hours . . . a piano would be provided, and singing allowed. This would permit talented New Zealanders both vocal and pianoforte, to express their national character. It would be better if such premises were away from main thoroughfares and busy streets, and placed in spacious areas with surrounding gardens . . . Unlicensed agents would not be necessary, and there would be no room for the sly grogger. Wine could be drunk in a restful atmosphere underneath the hand of the law, and not as at present, behind hedges and bullrushes.

By 1955 the country's vineyards were producing a half-million gallons of wine. But heavy imports and hardly diminished liquor trade disinterest had, year by year since the war, seriously weakened the local market for an industry with a £2,000,000 capital investment plus almost £1,000,000 in accumulated wine stocks. To assist this section of the economy the government in 1955 reduced the minimum quantity that might be sold by winemakers and wine resellers from two gallons to one quart bottle for wines under twenty-six per cent proof spirit and, as a temporary measure, lowered the minimum for fortified wines to half a gallon. This was later made permanent and also lowered to a single bottle but the industry was not to be rescued from its difficulties by this measure alone.

The following year, ten members of parliament (selected from both sides of the House) were appointed to a Winemaking Industry Committee with power to inquire into all aspects of the industry and its problems. They heard evidence, toured the wine districts, and, after several extensions of time, produced a report in September 1957, which has become an industry landmark.

'The attributes of the craftsman and the ingredients of success in winemaking,' their report stated, were 'honest and persistent endeavour, imagination, technical exactitude, with achievement as

Reforms Come at Last

the most coveted reward.' Fortunately, a series of practical reforms was recommended to give this paragon a fighting chance in his more worldly surroundings.

While the hotel trade had enjoyed monopoly rights to sale of wine by single bottles before 1955 — and used it to sell imported wines — they had also, after 1955, effectively blocked winemakers from establishing their own retail outlets.

The committee found that it had 'become difficult to obtain a wine-seller's licence, and exceedingly difficult to secure the grant of more than one or even a very few in any district' because the liquor trade always lodged objections. 'The most usual plea — almost an invariable one — is that the licence is not required as wine may be bought at existing hotels.'

In a declaration of far-reaching importance, the committee recommended: 'That wine-resellers' licences be more freely granted and that an application for such a licence should not be refused because of the existence or probable existence of other forms of licence, and that Licensing Committees be given a general direction to grant an application . . . '

Not only did the number of wine resellers' premises subsequently double (from 136 in 1957 to over 250 in 1964, mostly owned by winemakers) but also the public, finding New Zealand wine readily available for the first time — even making its acquaintance for the first time — increased consumption from 454,000 gallons in 1957 to 1,113,000 gallons in 1964. And the hotel trade was now pleased to offer New Zealand wines.

The £500,000 company formed by McWilliams Wines in 1962 included representatives of Ballins and New Zealand Breweries on the board of directors. Penfolds' £250,000 company registered in 1963 had forty per cent of its shares held by Dominion Breweries, an associate company of Leopard Breweries, Innes Industries Ltd, and various wine and spirit merchants. In 1964 Corbans expanded its shareholding to include ten wine and spirit merchants who had taken thirty per cent of the shares in their £350,000 company. The days were over when publicans poured sediment from one wine bottle to the next and shook their wines before serving.

Now that the pioneering is over the winemakers who combine the skills of primary producer, manufacturer and retailer in one small unit must still find time to be politicians. To protect their interest from embraces instead of blows there was increasing talk of organization through co-operatives. By the early 1960s a start had been made by the Viticultural Association, which had received a licence for experimental brandy-making on this basis. Ten years' successful operation of a co-operative still producing grape-spirit for fortifying the wines of eleven Henderson growers points to what could be achieved.

A modern winery can produce in a week what it took the Levets a lifetime to make on their crude press at the Lord Glasgow Vineyards. A nation's culture, like its technology, can make progress too. The 1957 select committee could see no harm in New Zealanders taking wine with their food in a public place, in carrying off a single bottle from a winemaker, or in tasting brandy made from the grapes of their own country. It was even unnecessary for the Department of Agriculture's research centre to masquerade under the name Te Kauwhata Horticultural Station and the committee recommended that it be renamed Te Kauwhata Viticultural Station.[3]

The committee repeated the eleven-year-old Royal Commission recommendation that wines be sold in restaurants. This came into effect in 1960. The legislation at first cautiously limited the number to be licensed throughout the country to ten but the following year the total was left to the discretion of the Licensing Control Commission. Raising a weird voice from the past, prohibitionists attempted to stop restaurants being granted liquor permits in no-licence districts: they were defeated in a Supreme Court action. By 1962 the Commission had granted seventeen licences and in its annual report could safely permit itself the comment: 'It is scarcely necessary to remark that the fears of some have proved groundless, that to legalize the sale of a very limited range of alcoholic beverages in selected restaurants would create or accentuate social evils.'

Distillation of beverage brandy, a natural corollary to winemaking also recommended by the 1957 committee and on countless other occasions, was initiated by the granting of experimental licences to

---

3. Popularly known as plain Te Kauwhata in any case, the station continued to offer the industry service in testing grape varieties and propagating them for sale and setting high standards of winemaking. No field days to demonstrate cellar techniques or vineyard management have been held since the early 1960s and it would be pleasant to imagine that this is because the industry has no need of such assistance.

six winemakers in 1964. No thunderbolts shattered the towers of their still-houses.

A modest beginning in industry co-ordination was made, as suggested in 1957, by a viticultural Advisory Committee comprising representatives from five government departments and three growers' organizations. Parallel to Easter Show wine judging run by the Department of Agriculture for many years, the Industries and Commerce Department, in co-operation with the Advisory Committee, began to organise an annual wine competition, the results of which were published in an illustrated booklet that also introduced the industry and its background to the public. Through its most successful television personality, the food and wine expert Graham Kerr, the state-owned Broadcasting Corporation introduced a breath of life to New Zealand kitchens and New Zealand wine took its place in tens of thousands of homes.

In the 1960s wine was being exported from Henderson to Canada and from Hawkes Bay to Australia, and New Zealand won numerous gold medals and other awards at international wine fairs in Europe.

Sales of New Zealand wine reached over the million-gallon mark for the first time in 1962–63, an increase of 140,000 gallons in one year. From the 1963 vintage, 155 winemakers put down a record 1,356,000 gallons. Forty-four of them produced all but 100,000 gallons of this from over 1000 acres of grapes.

Good wine had become available for every table. The product of the ripe clusters dreamed of by the first settlers was now within the reach of all.

Milan Erceg, Windy Hill Vineyards, Henderson.

A Kumeu planting.

Ross Spence, Matua Valley Wines, Waimauku.

Khaleel Corban.

Peter Babich and Peter Fredatovich, Lincoln Vineyards, Henderson.

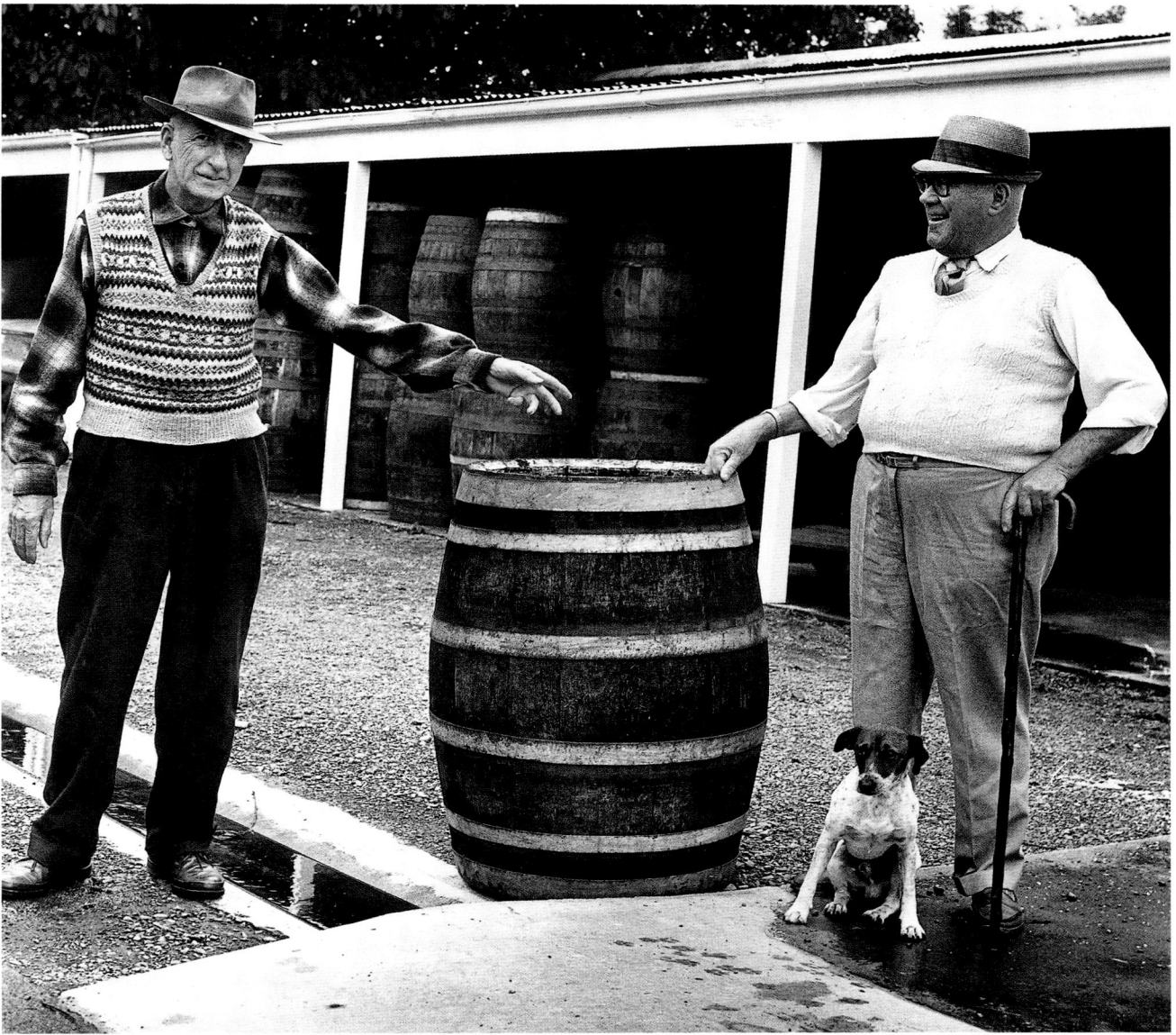

Frank and Cecil Vidal, Vidal Wines, Hawkes Bay.

Opposite
Corbans' Taupaki planting.

Opposite below
Corbans' Kumeu planting.

Leo Sim's winery, Himatangi.

Antonio Zame, Capri Vineyards, Gisborne.

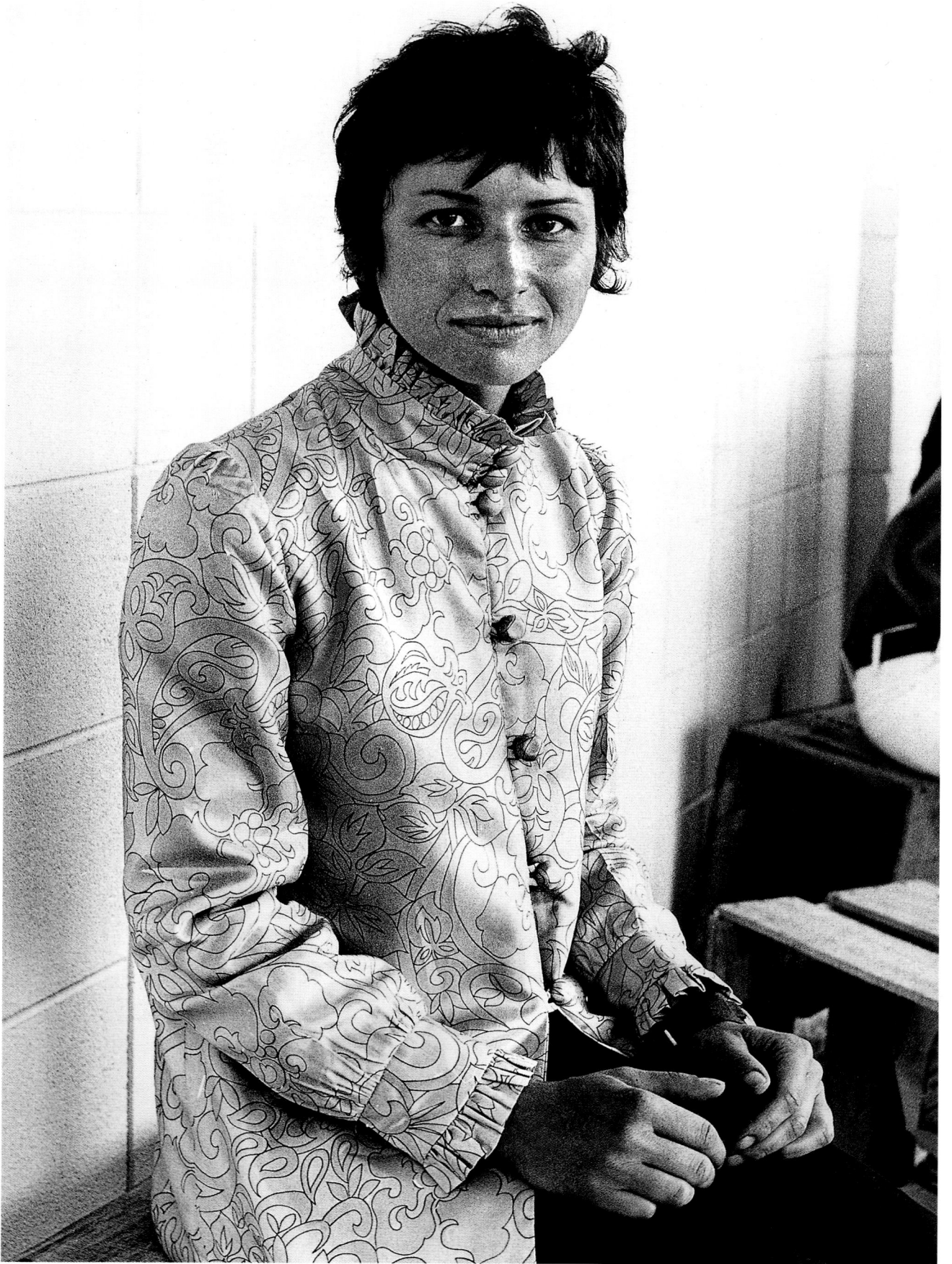

Milan Erceg, Windy Hill Vineyards, Henderson.

Opposite
Diana Balich, Golden Sunset Vineyards, Henderson.

Hawkes Bay pickers at day's end, McWilliams'
Te Awanga vineyard.

Opposite
Corbans' vineyard workers Jack Garner and Jim
Thompson sample the fruits of their labour.

Mate Brajkovich, San Marino Vineyards, Kumeu.

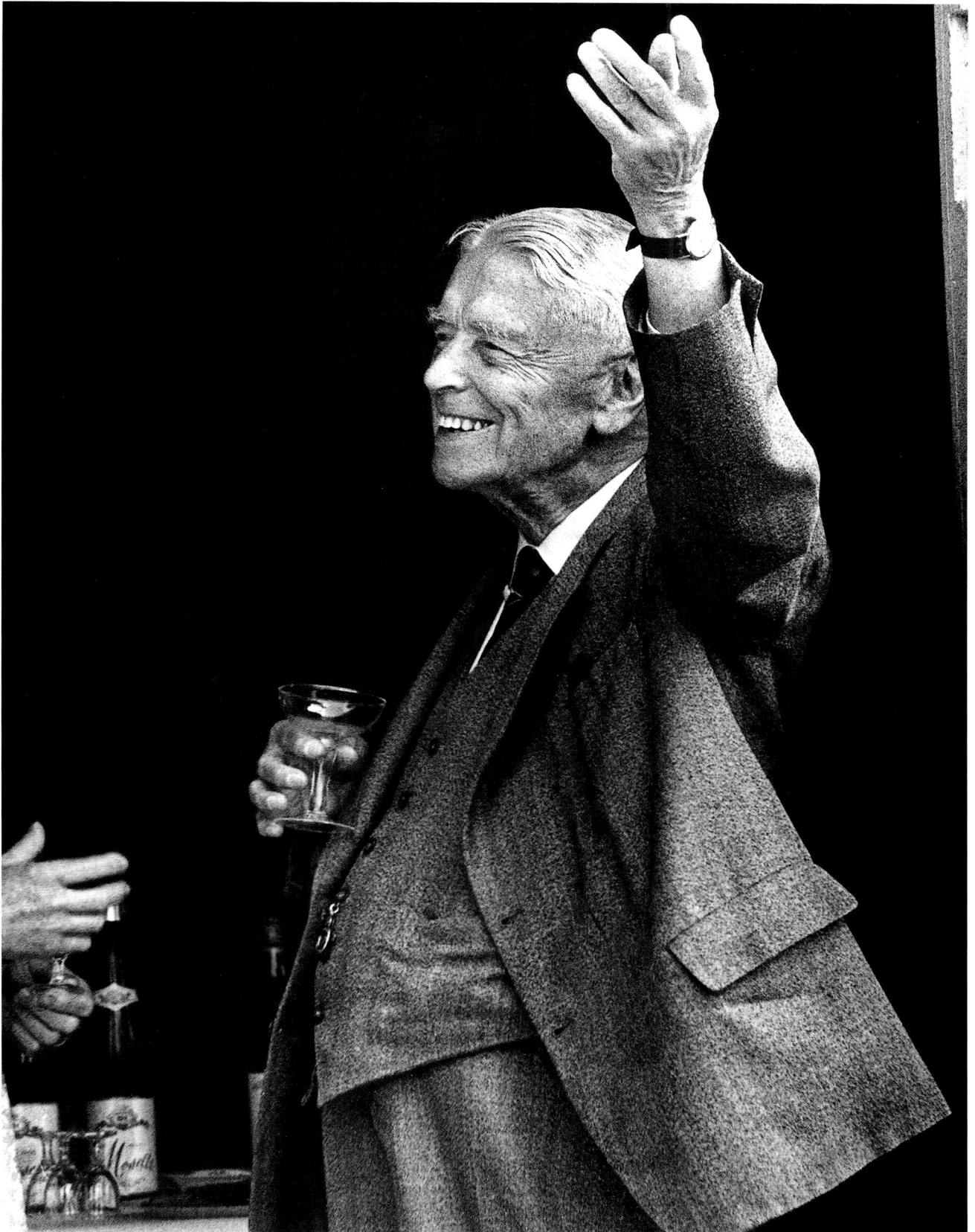

Walter Nash, former prime minister, enjoys the 1968 viticultural field day, a photograph widely reproduced on his death later that year.

A San Marino tasting.

OPPOSITE
A discerning customer (eighty-seven years
old) explores the Totara Vineyard range.

Mission students rescue classic grapes from the rain.

Opposite
Joseph Babich (right) and visitor, Babich's Vineyards, Henderson.

Opposite below
Brother Sylvester, Mission Vineyards, Hawkes Bay.

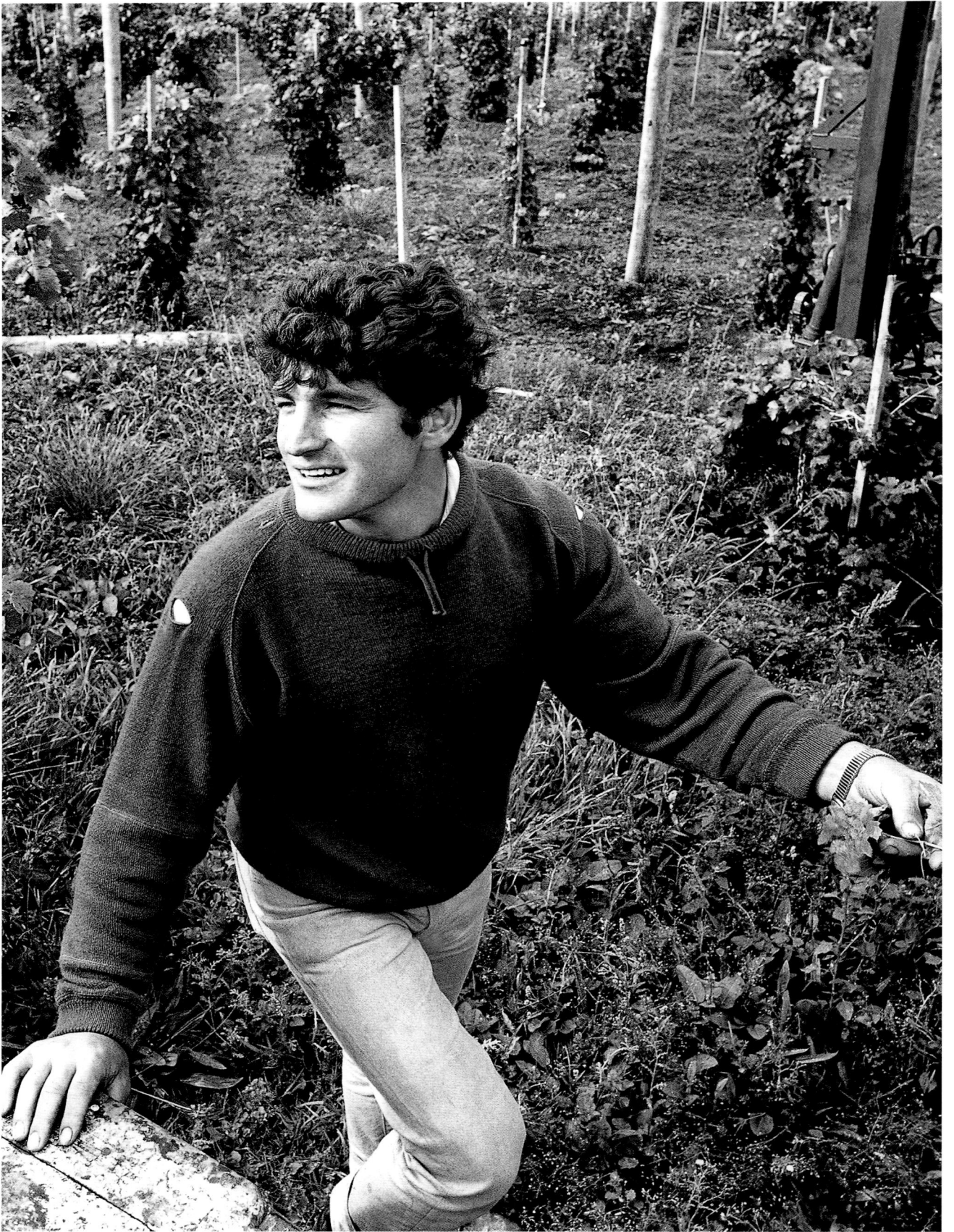

Nick Nobilo, Gilbey-Nobilo Wines, Huapai.

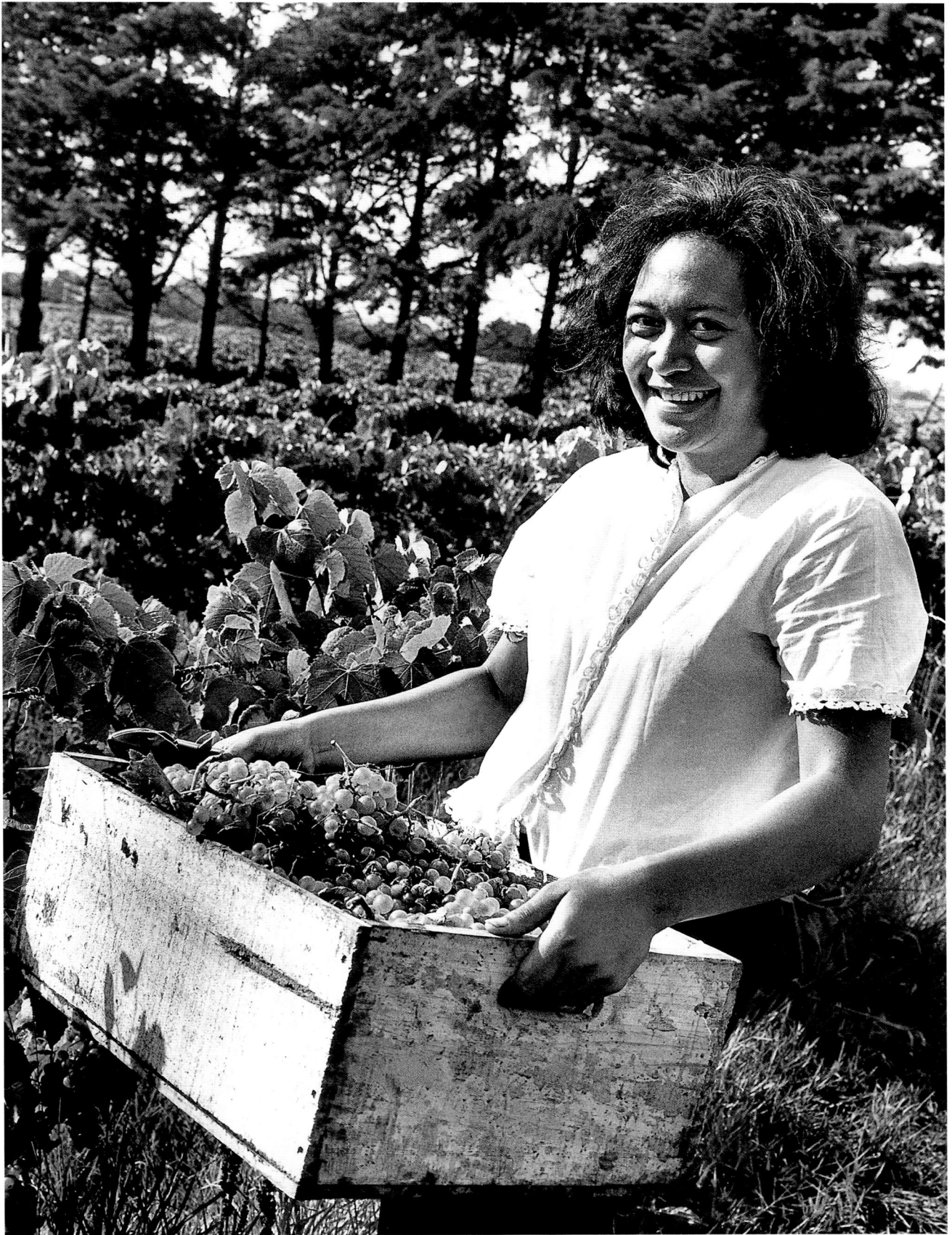

Elizabeth Ngaputa, Corbans' Mt Lebanon Vineyards.

Bruce Cameron, Corbans' Mt Lebanon Vineyards.

Totara Vineyards, Thames.

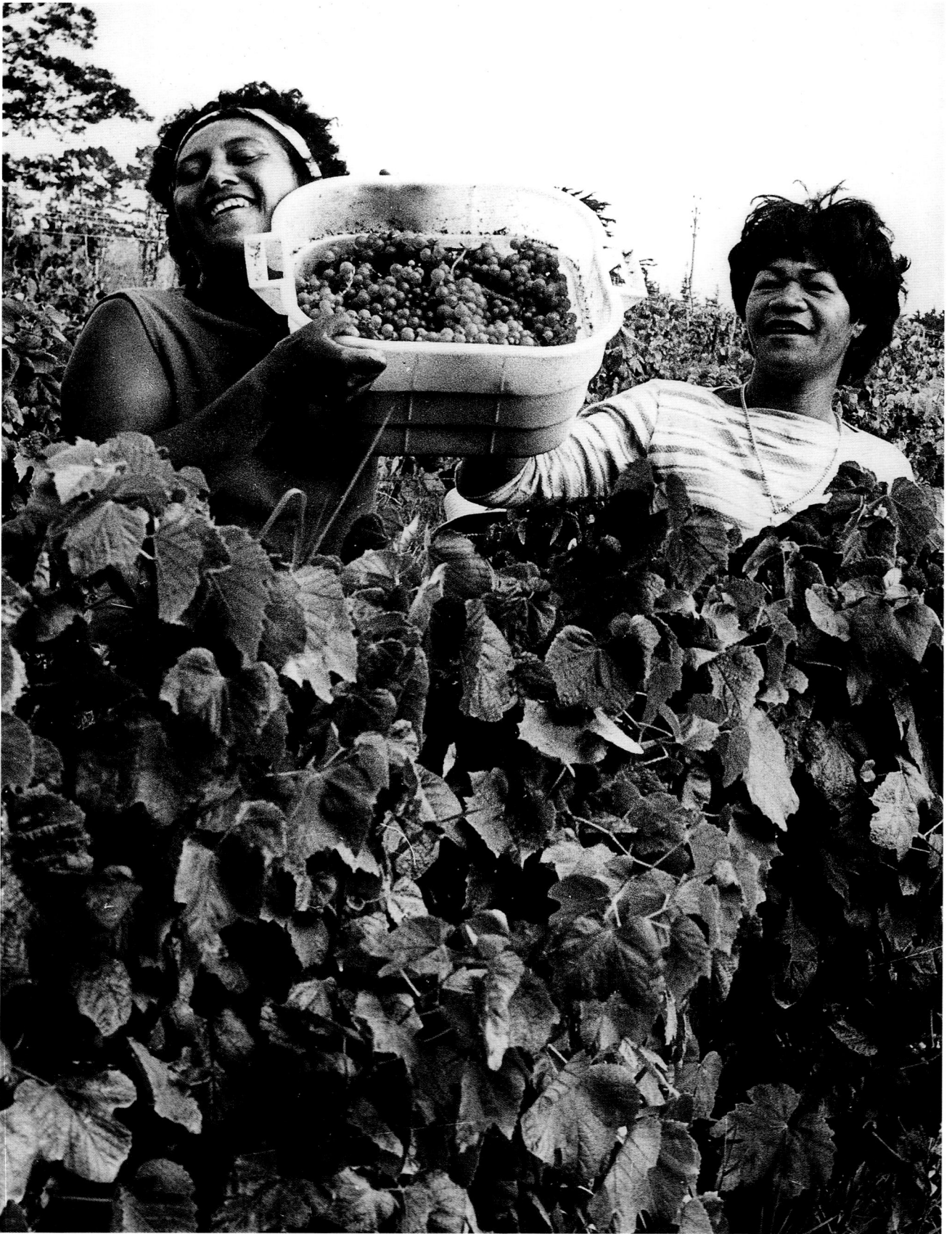

Revelling in the harvest, West Auckland.

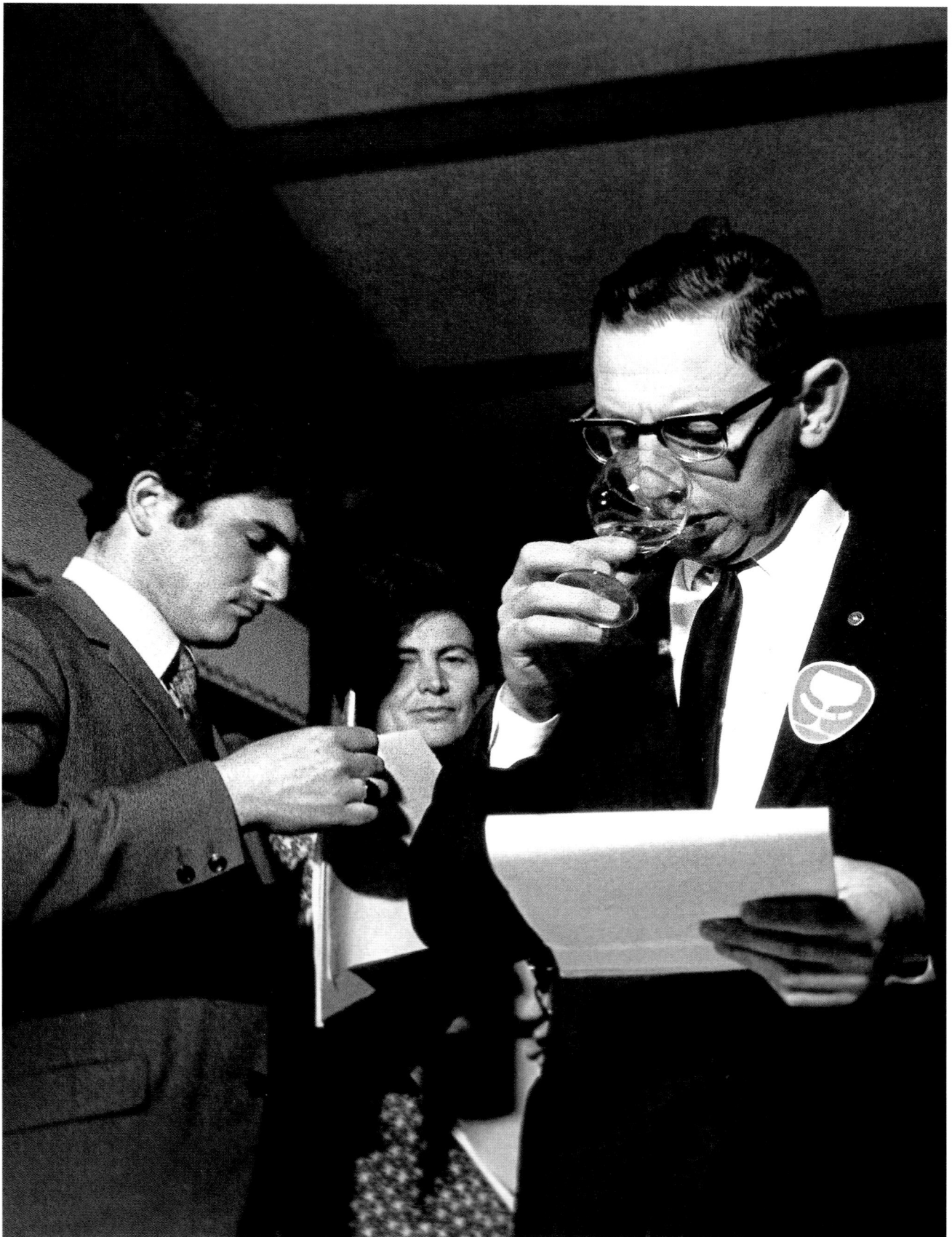

Assessing the product: Nick Nobilo and Alex Corban at a Connoisseurs' Club tasting.

Index

The index lists people named in the text. Page references for illustrations are in italics.